Stories for Talking

A programme to support the early development of language through storytime

by
Rebecca Bergmann

Illustrated by Kate Wood

A QEd Publication

Published in 2008
Reprinted 2012

ISBN 978 1 898873 54 9

British Library Cataloguing
A catalogue record for this book is available from the British Library.

Published by QEd Publications, 39 Weeping Cross, Stafford ST17 0DG
Tel: 01785 620364
Fax: 01785 607797
Website: www.qed.uk.com
Email: orders@qed.uk.com

Acknowledgements
Many thanks to Kate Wood for providing such wonderful illustrations to use with the activities, to Anne Hartley of Meynell School in Sheffield for providing inspiration, and to Chris Taylor and Nick Bergmann for all their practical support.

Contents

Introduction

There are so many more children now with language difficulties

Why are children entering nursery with poorer language skills?

What can we do about this problem of poor speech and language?

Ofsted have highlighted speaking and listening as our weakest area again

There's no way he is ready for the demands of the literacy hour

These are the frequently heard concerns of early years practitioners. There is plenty of anecdotal evidence regarding the increasing numbers of children who are experiencing language difficulties, however, the same concerns are being echoed at a strategic level – Ofsted reports frequently highlight concerns around 'speaking and listening' above other areas of the curriculum. The Bercow Report (2008) has given formal recognition to the significant numbers of children nationally with speech, language and communication needs.

There is an growing recognition of the importance of language in both social and educational development, particularly in the early years, that has far reaching long-term effects on individuals well into adult life. A significant body of research has indicated the effect language difficulties has on behaviour, self-esteem, social skills and relationships (Lindsay et al, 2008; Jerome et al, 2002; Redmond & Rice, 2002). The Bercow Report (2008) states 'The ability to communicate is an essential life skill for all children and young people and it underpins a child's social, emotional and educational development'.

Clearly there is a significant problem, with evidence to suggest it is growing. In order to address this, many programmes designed to increase children's language and interaction skills have been devised – some extremely effective and easy to implement, others requiring a lot of extra time, staff or specialist skills. Many early years practitioners report that, alongside other pressures, they are not able to implement many programmes which require specific allocated time and extra staffing, and yet they recognise the need for some children to receive targeted, specific activities and programmes. With this in mind a practical, accessible programme was devised to increase children's language and interaction skills in the early years.

Stories for Talking

The *Stories for Talking* approach was inspired by an early years practitioner working in a setting with high levels of deprivation and language need, who recognised the urgent needs of these children, yet felt limited in what could be offered on a regular basis.

The aim was to use simple and effective methods that could help *all* children (with and without language difficulties), in a structured format that staff could easily implement. It therefore provides a prescriptive tool for those who feel they need it, yet a flexible 'ethos' for those who feel confident in applying the principles.

The approach is based on storytime, simply using the normal daily activity and staffing already in place in any nursery setting. So there are no additional demands that implementing new programmes can present. By using storytime it enables a small group approach that is intensive (daily) and interactive. It is highly structured and repetitive, using very familiar and popular children's stories from which topic vocabulary and activities emerge. The approach is inclusive, providing equal opportunities for children with special educational needs to access a daily activity with their peers. Partnership with parents is also encouraged, where learning can be reinforced and parents made to feel their role is just as important in the process.

The children who benefit most from this approach are primarily those who are showing signs of language delay; children from deprived areas who often show early signs of impoverished language skills; and those learning English as an additional language will benefit enormously. In addition, children with very severe language difficulties such as Specific Language Impairment, would also benefit from this approach, due to the simple level it starts at and the highly repetitive and structured programme of activities. Children with general learning difficulties and with mild-moderate social interaction/Autistic Spectrum Disorder may also benefit, but may need extra support to access the group activities. Children who have normally developing language skills, but who are socially withdrawn, can also benefit from the confidence building, social experience of this approach.

While *Stories for Talking* targets those with difficulties, it is likely that *all* children would benefit. Many of the Early Learning Goals within the Early Years Foundation Stage (EYFS) are covered, particularly in the 'Communication, Language and Literacy' and 'Personal, Social and Emotional' areas of learning. It aims to partner speech and language therapy approaches into storytime and play experiences, and to provide early years practitioners with effective skills to develop all children's language and learning.

Chapter 1   Storytime – Friend or Foe?

Imagine . . . you are a 3 year-old. You've not been at nursery for long, and you have language difficulties. That means you have difficulty understanding language, you struggle to listen and maintain concentration, you don't have very many words and have difficulty recalling the words you do know . . . and find it hard to put sentences together.

It's late in the morning, you've had a busy time. The teacher says something to the whole class but you don't catch it. The others are starting to move towards the carpet area. You decide to follow, but when you get there, there is only room at the back of the area. Aha! You see there is space next to that boy you often sit near to – he's friendly and you often play with him – you decide to sit next to him.

The teacher begins to read a story. You don't understand what she's saying but the pictures are quite interesting. After a while though you get a bit fed up with stretching your neck to see around and over all the children in front of you. The Velcro on your shoe is undone – better fix that – do it up, not quite straight, undo, do it up, not quite right, undo – uh oh . . . the teacher's looking at you and saying something! Oh no . . . it looks like you're in trouble. You'll just try and look at the pictures again.

You watch for a bit and then the teacher looks up and says something. You don't know what she said but it looks like she's asking a question. Everyone else is putting their hand up so you do the same. The teacher looks at you and says your name. Oh no! She wants an answer to something! You don't understand . . . er . . . er . . . er . . . oh, you can see a picture of a dog on the page of the book, and you know that word, so you say 'dog'. The whole class starts laughing, 'Great', you think! 'I've cracked a joke! Everyone thinks I'm funny' so you say it again. Everyone laughs even louder . . . except the teacher. She looks cross and says 'no' to you, followed by something else and then asks a different child. Oh dear! You must have got it wrong.

Never mind, the ribbons and hair slide of the girl in front look really interesting so you decide to have a look at those. She turns around and smiles. Great! The boy next to you is a bit fidgety too so he plays with the ribbons. The three of you have quite a giggle and begin a tickling game – this is much more fun and you're good at this. But . . . oh no you're in trouble again . . . oh dear, the teacher's pointing at the front of the group next to her chair. Oh no, you've go to move. She looks so cross.

You go and sit right beside her chair, but in order to see the pictures you have to really crick your head back and your neck's hurting. You're tired. In fact you're hungry too. You begin to wonder when your mum is coming . . . and what you will have for lunch . . . and what you will do this afternoon.

Great! At last it's finished. Everybody's moving and the book's on the shelf. At last that's over!

Sadly, this is how storytime really is for many children with language difficulties. It is not the shared enjoyment of wonderful stories that so many other children are able to enjoy.

The use of books and stories are excellent ways of developing vocabulary, widening experiences, fostering imagination and creativity, introducing sequence and narrative, exploring different options and outcomes, and providing examples of problem solving. These are the beginnings of the journey of literacy.

So, how can we help a child with the problems described in the earlier example? The very activity that *could* help these children with language difficulties is, in fact, the one that proves to be hardest. This turns them off – possibly for life, with far reaching implications if we don't get it right.

Let us unpick the scenario and see how we could have made it easier for this child.

The structure and nature of storytime

1. Timing
Storytime is often placed late in the day or at the very end of a nursery session. Often after an active, stimulating and demanding day, children are tired and easily distracted. If they have difficulties with attention, listening and language, the whole session will be even more demanding.
- *Try different times of the day for storytime, bearing in mind that your intention should be to enthuse and captivate young minds.*

2. The size of the group
The child in the example above struggled to find a space and to see the book – a bad start for any child at storytime. But if you need to see the pictures because you do not *understand* the words being spoken, it is even more important that you are part of a smaller group. If possible, try and have groups of varying sizes, the weaker children being in a smaller group (possibly 6-8 children), and the more able children being in larger groups. Obviously, the number of groups you can have will depend on your staffing levels.
- *You will need all staff members to be involved in storytime, each taking their own group.*
- *Have smaller groups for storytime – grouped according to ability and with all staff involved.*

3. Position
This may seem a small point, but it is *very* important. Make sure every child can see the book. A child sitting too far away, or too close for that matter, way off to the side and struggling to see what others can see quite easily is going to lose interest, feel left out and will, very likely, begin to distract others.
- *Position your small group carefully in front of the book and check that they can all see clearly.*

4. Language level of the story
The child in our scenario clearly did not understand much of the story, nor the questions about it. It is really important that you choose a story with really simple language for those

children with language difficulties. Pictures do help greatly, but be aware also that some books, while having beautiful and numerous pictures, still have long passages of text that can present real difficulties for some children.

- *For children with language difficulties, start with really basic books – those you might consider too young for nursery-aged children. Once you are confident the children are accessing the story and understanding the words, you can gradually move on to more complex stories.*

5. Illustrations

The child in our example completely relied on the pictures to get him through storytime. This is how it is for many children with language difficulties. All children benefit and learn more from stories where what they hear is backed up by what they see. Children love colourful pictures, so it is important to use them effectively. Point to the appropriate bit of the picture to help children with problems understanding – to help them to link the words and the pictures together.

- *So choose books with lots of large, clear pictures and pictures that illustrate key aspects of the text.*

6. Repetition

The child in our example could hardly wait until storytime was over. He expects to fail. He has no sense of anything being familiar or of success. Every day he finds he cannot understand the words and gets confused. This is because very often he is presented with a new story.

Repetition is *critical* to learning language for any child – and particularly for those who have language difficulties. Familiarity breeds confidence and a foundation to begin to build new skills upon. All children gain a great deal from hearing the same story many times. In fact, they very rarely need prompting from us. How many times do we hear them asking for the same stories over and over again? Children with language difficulties particularly need a story to be repeated many times, preferably on consecutive days to help them retain and build on the new language they have learned.

In the *Stories for Talking* approach, each story is read and used for language work for a minimum of one week, and could easily be spread over two, with repetition of the activities. However, you need to be flexible – if you feel it would benefit the children, and have activities up your sleeve, extend it for longer still.

- *Same story, read daily, for at least a week.*

7. Structure and nature of the story

A lot of story books written for pre-schoolers fall generally into two categories. Firstly, there are those that describe a whole sequence of events. The Alfie series by Shirley Hughes are examples. The story evolves as a sequence of events over time, possibly with a problem to solve along the way. In general, little repetition of language is used. The language involved can be fairly complex (particularly for children with language difficulties) and there is a fair proportion of text to every picture. These types of stories are enjoyed by children with reasonably competent levels of language. Other examples of these types of stories include the Apple Tree Farm series by Heather Amery and the Thomas series by Rev. W. Awdrey.

The second category are those in which particular actions are repeated frequently. Examples include *The Hungry Caterpillar* by Eric Carle and *Oh Dear* (Buster collecting the eggs) by Rod Campbell. The 'interest' is created by this action being repeated by different characters or with different objects. Generally these stories have simple language and less text per picture and page.

In the author's experience, and in many observations of children with language difficulties at storytime, it is this second category of story that tends to keep their interest and give them more enjoyment. They are easier to understand with lots of pictures, with less and simpler language. It is easy to get the gist of where the story is going due to their repetitive nature. In addition, they have the advantage of enabling a child with language difficulties to learn new words by topic. Stories of this type are used in the *Stories for Talking* programme.

- *Be mindful of the type of story you choose for children with language difficulties. Choose repetitive, simple stories.*

Summary

In summary then, this is what is recommended for a successful storytime:
- Hold your storytime early on in the day.
- Have smaller groups (if possible) of similar ability children, with no more than 6-8 children in the lower ability group.
- Sit the children where they can easily see the book.
- Keep the language/text simple, with not much per page.
- Use stories with lots of big, clear illustrations that reflect the key details of each page.
- Read the same story every day for a week.
- Choose stories that have a repetitive structure.

Chapter 2 It's so complex – what is most important?

Learning and using language is one of the most complex tasks our brains ever achieve. The more that is learned about language, the more we realise how many different processes and skills are required. It is quite astounding that so many of us do develop language so easily and that babies begin this process at such a very early stage.

Many of you will have come across children who have been described as having 'speech and language difficulties', yet many of them present difficulties very differently. This is because there are so many different aspects of language acquisition that can 'go wrong'. Not surprisingly, many early years practitioners find children with speech and language difficulties quite a mystery. Not only do these children rarely present the same way, sometimes they have language difficulties but good skills in all other areas of development.

The approach suggested in this book is *not* designed to be a 'cure-all' for the many different types of speech and language difficulties. However, it does focus on many of the core skills needed to be able to develop language. This chapter describes the core skills required in this process.

Core aspects of language

The core aspects of language include comprehension of language, expressive language, semantics, functional use of language, and attention and listening skills. It is worth considering each of these briefly in turn.

1. Comprehension of language

Comprehension, or the understanding of language, is absolutely crucial to developing effective spoken language skills and many aspects of learning and yet this is an area of difficulty that is not readily identified. Many parents confidently report that their child 'understands everything'. Early years practitioners will often have noticed the child's lack of spoken language before their lack of understanding. With some children it is very obvious that most of what you are saying is not being understood. However, many children become so adept at reading all the clues in their environment, and so *appear* to understand the language (they are watching where your eyes are pointing, your gestures, what the other children are doing, using their knowledge of routines). In some cases, they have good understanding, but more often than not, children with poor talking or 'expressive skills' have difficulties with comprehension too.

Usually, weak understanding underpins poor talking, so it is really important that we work on comprehension of language at the same time, if not before, expressive language.

That is why, in the weekly plans of activities that follow each story in the *Stories of Talking* programme, the comprehension activity always comes before the talking activity – so don't plan on doing Friday's activity before Tuesday's – there is sound logic to the plans!

Remember – understanding *before* talking.

2. Expressive language

Expressive language, or talking, is much easier to spot when it is not developing correctly. Generally, this is the aspect that gives most concern to the parent or early years practitioner. It may be the child has only developed a few words or has a good range of words but does not put them together in sentences.

The *Stories for Talking* approach works on both aspects of expressive language:
- building up the number of words in the child's talking repertoire (developing their 'vocabulary');
- helping them learn how to put words together in the right way to build up phrases and sentences (developing their 'grammatical skills').

Depending on which level you choose to work at, you can help children build vocabulary, construct sentences or learn to tell stories.

3. Semantics

Semantics is another word for word meanings. In this context it refers to us helping children to build up knowledge about the attributes of objects. When we have a full understanding of a word, we can then store it in the correct part of our giant-sized 'dictionary' in our head where we keep all the words we know.

For example, the word 'cow' will be stored in your 'brain dictionary' in the 'farm animals' section. That is because you know all about a cow – it has 4 legs, a tail, a head, an udder, has horns, eats grass, lives on a farm . . . and it will be stored along with words such as 'pig', 'sheep', 'goat', 'hen', 'horse' etc. because they have a lot of features in common. You can only store it here because you have all that knowledge – that knowledge provides a 'web' of information that gives you its full word meaning and links it to other word meanings. All the related words are held together by their 'webs' or 'semantic connections'.

When we build up our 'dictionaries' in a systematic format where related words are stored together, it helps speed up word retrieval. In other words, when you need a word to say something, you can find it more easily from your 'brain dictionary' when it is stored in the correct place. Here is an analogy:

You go to your library to find a travel guide on Spain to help you plan your holiday. When you get to the library, you find that they have employed a librarian who has done away with the ordered system. You have to hunt in every section, on every shelf, through every book to try and find the one you need. In the end you give up as you cannot find it.

This is rather like children with a language difficulty. As well as having only a few words, they often have poor semantic skills too. All the words they know are just stored in a random, unrelated heap in their 'dictionaries'. And so, when they try to find the word they need, they either take a long time to recall it or cannot think of it at all. This is called a word finding difficulty.

Going back to the example of the library, you hear that a new librarian has had some training on categorising and systematically storing the books. You go in again – straight to the travel section, European shelf, Spanish section – and within one minute you have found the book you need.

By teaching new vocabulary using a semantic framework, that is, using topics to teach related words together, we are helping children both learn and store new words efficiently, which will help them find the right word quickly.

That is why the stories chosen in *Stories for Talking* are topic-based stories, and the activities related to the story focus on choosing topic-related words.

4. Functional use of language (known as 'Pragmatics')

Having a good understanding, good vocabulary, lots of sentences and an ability to retell a story is not very helpful if we do not put them to use in our everyday lives to make requests, give directions, comment on things, ask questions and take turns in a conversation.

Some children with Autistic Spectrum Disorders have these types of social interaction difficulties as part of a broader profile of difficulties with non-verbal communication, social interaction and behaviour. However, other children are reluctant to use language *functionally* with others due to a lack of confidence, poor self-esteem or a history of never having enough time to speak before somebody else jumps in and interrupts them. The activities in *Stories for Talking* include many opportunities for these children to use their newly acquired words and sentences to interact with each other – taking turns, listening to each other, giving each other messages and so on. This interaction will enable them to develop the necessary skills and confidence in functionally using their language.

5. Attention and listening skills

While 'attention' and 'listening' are not strictly language skills, they are fundamental to learning language. If we are not paying attention and listening fully, we do not hear and do not learn language. So it is really important that we set up storytime to help children to pay attention and listen – a quiet room or area will help prevent distractions.

Chapter 3 Children with language difficulties – supporting strategies

The strategies discussed in this chapter can be used at any time, and are particularly effective when used in play and interaction all around the nursery as well as in storytime groups.

The following analogy can help us see the value of these strategies and helps us see just how hard it is for children with language difficulties.

You are holidaying in Spain and you do not know any of the language. On the first night you go to a restaurant where the waiter does not speak any English. He speaks to you, but you haven't got a clue what he's talking about.

What would help in this situation? Would it help if he just kept repeating himself – the same fast and lengthy 'gabble' he spoke before? Would it help if he spoke louder – or even shouted? Would it help if he came up close and spoke very slowly, overemphasising the production of each and every word as if . . . you . . . were . . . deaf? Obviously none of these strategies would help, but what if (a) he gave you the menu to look at; (b) used gestures to show you that one page was the drinks menu and the other page was the food; and (c) alerted you to the photos on the menu showing what each dish looked like? This would obviously be a lot more helpful. These are all forms of *visual supports.*

Visual supports

We can provide visual support by using objects, pictures, photos, symbols, signs, natural gestures. Using visual supports gives children who have difficulties a better chance of grasping what is being said, rather than being lost in a world of 'foreign' language.

Ideas for visual supports are provided in the storytime activities, but you could also begin to think of ways to support these children around the rest of the nursery for example:
- use pictures or symbols to support your instructions telling the children when it's time for snack, outdoor play, story etc.;
- use real objects and demonstrate, as well as explain, what you would like the children to do, for example, in a craft activity;
- have photos or examples of work done by the children, when you're talking about a trip or an activity you have been doing;
- have objects, pictures or symbols available to the whole group so that a child with little language can point to a picture to answer your question or take part in the conversation;
- put up symbols on velcro in the different areas of the nursery (for example, a painting symbol in the painting area) so that a child with little language can use a picture to take to his friend to ask him to play. This will help prevent social exclusion for a child with little language.

Using symbols with children with language difficulties is an increasingly popular and effective way of working. They are used both to compensate for lack of understanding and talking, but also to teach skills and prevent later difficulties with conversational skills (*Communicate: In Print 2* is a symbol software package frequently used by speech and language therapists and educational settings – see details on page 15).

Adapting your language

Returning to the Spanish waiter – you have been on holiday for a few days and are beginning to get the hang of a few words and phrases, but you are by no means proficient at the language. When he speaks rapidly, you are still very confused, but what if (a) he speaks in short, simple, sentences; (b) speaks slowly; (c) leaves a pause in between phrases to give you time to process one bit of information before he gives you the next; and (d) repeats the sentence again if it's clear you have not understood. These are all strategies you can use to help children understand what you are saying.

Take time to really try and adapt your language:
- Use simple language – no long, complicated words; no hard concepts (for example, 'before'); no hard grammatical words (such as 'if', 'when', 'only'); keep sentences short.
- Speak a bit more slowly than you normally do.
- Leave some gaps between sentences. Pause to allow the children time to process the language already spoken.
- Repeat the sentence again if necessary. Do not keep changing the sentence (unless you have just realised it was too complex). If you change the format or wording of the sentence, the child has to begin trying to process a whole new sentence time and time again and gets nowhere.

By the end of the holiday, you are on good terms with the waiter and he is doing his best to try and teach you some Spanish. To start with you were lost and couldn't pick out any words from the stream of sounds that came from his lips. However, he recognised your difficulty and began to use objects to label as single words (he realised he needed visuals), and would give you words or simple phrases to match objects or events around the restaurant. When you became brave and said a word, he would add another word to it to help you build a little phrase. Your confidence grew . . . and so did your Spanish!

So, in order to help children learn expressive language, you need to be armed with your visuals and use modelling and expansion strategies as explained below.

Modelling language

While playing with a child, use words or short sentences at the next level the child needs to move on to. If Johnny has no words, you will use single words to encourage him to copy. If Mary has some single words, you will model two word phrases for her to try to copy. If Mohammed has simple two word phrases you will model three word sentences for him to copy.

Expand language

If a child has some language and says something to you, you will say the same word or phrase back to them, but add one more word on. For example:

- Mary says 'car', adult says 'yes, **Daddy's** car';
- Mohammed says 'big dog', adult says 'yes, big dog's **eating**';
- Anna says 'wearing boots', adult says, 'oh yes, **Anna's** wearing boots';
- Raheem says 'boy flying a kite', adult says, 'that boy's flying a **blue** kite'.

Using these strategies immerses the child in language that is accessible to them, but is also moving them on to the next stage. They are particularly effective in everyday activities around the nursery as you are playing with the children, commenting on what they are doing and responding to their attempts to interact with you. (**Further information and training on using strategies such as these are available from the Hanen Centre.)

Generalising skills into a variety of contexts

Having new words and phrases is an important start, but in order for children to learn language effectively, they need to have many more opportunities to continue learning and practise using their skills in a whole variety of different everyday settings.

So we need to set up other activities around the nursery which continues the topic we have been exploring in the storytime session. At the end of each activity section for each of the stories in the *Stories for Talking* programme, there are ideas for extending the topic into other curriculum areas. If a topic is continued into other curriculum areas it allows for:

- **Lots of repetition** – the more times that the children hear the language and have an opportunity to practise saying those new words and sentences, the more likely they are to retain them, thus allowing for greater confidence and progress.

- **Improved semantic development** – if a child is only shown one example of an object representing that new word you are teaching, they may think that word only applies to that specific object. The more examples of the same thing that s/he sees, the more likely s/he is to build up accurate semantic webs. For example, Sarah needs to know that the small, grey, plastic thing she has learned is a 'cat' in storytime has the same name as the big, black furry thing in the home corner, and the same name as Grandma's real ginger, stripy thing which is also known as 'Sid.'

- **Opportunities for functional use of language** – it is so encouraging when we see children learning new skills, and even better when we see those new skills enhancing and empowering children's lives. How rewarding for a child who has learned the names of 'food' in his storytime activities, to also be able to request his choice of snack, and join in with the game of 'café' in the role play area. Increasing the opportunities children have to use these new skills is vital to their development.

* *Communicate: In Print 2* Widgit Software, 124 Cambridge Science Park, Milton Road, Cambridge CB4 0ZS (www.widgit.com)
** The Hanen Centre, Suite 515-1075 Bay Street, Toronto, Ontario, Canada M5S 2B1 (www.hanen.org)

Chapter 4: So many words! Where do I start? A framework

Different types of words

The *Stories for Talking* approach is based on teaching a small number of different types of words related to a topic that emerges from the story. The different types of words or word classes that provide the basic building blocks in this approach are nouns, verbs, concepts and adjectives.

1. Nouns

These are *object* words such as 'car', 'teddy', 'mummy', 'banana', 'ball'. Words for objects are usually some of a child's first words and are generally easier to learn. This is because objects are very tangible – you can usually handle them, they are permanent, they exist for a long time and you can keep returning to them. Adults tend to tell children the names for 'things' far more frequently than other types of words. Watch an adult looking through a book with a young child and notice how many 'things' they point out and label (for example, 'boy' . . . 'icecream' . . . 'chair') as opposed to talking about what they are doing (such as 'eating' . . . 'sitting').

Nouns are obviously important and, being easier to learn, give a child a good start in building up their word bank or 'vocabulary'. So, in this approach we teach lots of nouns – 10 nouns for every topic/story taught.

2. Verbs

These are *action* words telling us what somebody or something is doing, such as 'eating', 'jumping', 'swimming', 'talking', 'sleeping'. Generally these words are harder to learn and come after object words, but for children with language difficulties they pose a particular problem and are often the reason why these children get stuck with language and fail to go on to speak in sentences. Why are they more difficult? Because they are much more abstract than objects – you can't reach out and touch an action. Often they happen quickly and then the action is finished. In picture form you cannot see them at all and children struggle to recognise which bit of an event relates to the action word.

Imagine you are a young child looking at a picture. An adult tells you: 'It's a boy kicking a ball'. You break the sentence down and realise there are three important words that you need to look for and 'map' onto the various bits of the picture: 'boy' . . 'kicking' . . 'ball'. You can see the 'boy', you can see the 'ball', but where is the 'kicking'? There is nothing to represent that word. The adult then points outside to a boy kicking a ball and says the sentence again. Still you can see a ball and a boy, but nothing to represent a 'kicking'. It is only when she says 'kicking' and does an action with that word – it is the movement of her leg and that boy's leg that must match that word kicking. The picture continues to be confusing to you as that leg doesn't wave about, it stays still, and yet she's still calling that kicking too!

Is it any wonder verbs are harder for children to learn? Add to that the fact mentioned earlier that we tend to talk about actions far less than we talk about objects, so children get less chance to hear action words and begin to unravel their mystery.

As this example demonstrated, using gesture and actions can help children to be able to 'map' verb words onto the right part of the picture or event. Using noises can also help. For example, you tell a child 'the girl is eating a sausage' – the child can see the 'girl', can see the 'sausage', but where is the 'eating'? If you pretend to eat using both gesture and eating noises while saying the word 'eating', repeating this lots of times, the child is much more likely to realise what the action word 'eating' is.

Verbs are essential to language development – every sentence needs some type of verb to 'hang' all of the other words around. So in this approach we make sure that we teach verbs as well as nouns, but only five per topic/story as they are harder.

3. Concepts (adjectives)

Adjectives are types of concepts that describe objects such as 'big', 'blue', 'dirty', 'long', 'spotty'. These words are more abstract – they are an aspect of an object, not a tangible object in itself. You can imagine a child hearing the sentence, 'You've got a big spoon', and thinking, 'I can see the spoon, but where's the 'big'?', before they know that 'big' is just a word to describe something about the spoon.

Once again using gesture, or signing, can really help. If you use your hands, facial expression and tone of voice every time you say 'big' the child begins to link the two together. Go round the nursery talking about everything that is 'big', such as 'big teddy', 'big car', 'big book' and they then begin to realise that all those things are not called a 'big', but because you wave your hands around the same way each time, they begin to recognise the pattern – they are the things which are bigger.

This is especially effective if you always compare the 'big' things to the 'little' things. If we don't have anything to compare something to then how do we know it is 'big' – it's only 'big' if there's something else that is 'little'. For this reason, and as a general rule, it is best to teach concepts in pairs. So as you go round the nursery looking at things that are 'big', try to make sure there's a little version of it on hand so that you can contrast it with 'little' – and don't forget to do a gesture/sign and use a different tone of voice for 'little' too. You can see how setting up your nursery activities to support the language taught in the story session is really crucial to children gaining a full understanding of the words.

Concepts are complex and their level of abstractness means that they need lots of teaching in a variety of settings using different practical examples. So in this approach we only teach two concepts (usually a pair of opposites) per story/topic.

Putting words together

With these three different types of words in their word bank, or 'vocabulary', children are now armed with the basic building blocks to begin building sentences. The three different types of words enable children to begin to build short sentences at first, and then gradually by adding one of the different word classes at a time they can make them longer and more detailed. For example:

- a noun and a verb – mouse (is) eating;
- a verb and a noun – eating (an) apple;
- put it together – noun, verb, noun: (the) mouse (is) eating (an) apple;
- add a concept – noun, verb, concept, noun: (the) mouse (is) eating (a) red apple;
- add another concept – concept, noun, verb, concept, noun: the little mouse is eating a red apple.

By this stage they will probably be able to change the order of the building blocks around to make different types of sentences such as: 'The mouse is little' and 'The apple is red'.

In the examples above, the little grammatical words such as 'the', 'is' and 'a' are in brackets because usually children who are at such a basic level of sentence building are not able to use these words. Most children will begin to acquire them as they become more competent with language and will naturally begin to insert them into their sentences. However, children with severe language difficulties struggle more in acquiring these words and an understanding of where to put them in a sentence.

Choosing the words for each topic

We have our story in front of us, so now we need to choose a topic and pick our 10 nouns, 5 verbs and 2 concepts. How do we go about it? Three essential principles that we always need to apply are frequency, function and semantics.

1. Frequency

Always choose 'high frequency' words. In other words, choose words that are common, frequently used words which children will hear, see and experience in their daily lives. Common sense tells us that we would teach a child the word 'dog' before 'antelope'. Try to think in this way when choosing words for each of the different word classes. The words do not have to be easy to say – it is familiarity that is important. For example, 'chocolate' is harder to say than 'leek' but is more well known.

2. Function

Also bear in mind which words might be most useful to a child practically. Not only is 'chocolate' more well known than 'leek', it is also a lot more motivating to learn! For each of the word classes try to choose words that are functional and useful. Imagine you had had an accident and did not get to the toilet in time – how much more useful it would be to have the concept of 'wet' in your vocabulary rather than 'blue'! We seem to be so obsessed with teaching children the concept of colours from such a young age when they generally are not very useful in practical situations. This is especially so if you are a child with language difficulties with only a handful of words to try to get your message across.

3. Semantics

It is essential that the words chosen are related to each other by topic. This firstly helps the child to organise their new words efficiently in their brain so that when they next go to find that word in their ever growing 'dictionary', they can find the word more easily.

It also helps children when they come to build sentences. Teaching children words that are related by topic is like providing them with building blocks with glue on – they more easily go together with the other words and make sentence building an easier task. For example, if you have been taught the words 'girl', 'eating' and 'sausage' it is easier to try and build a sentence than if you had been taught 'girl', 'climbing' and 'pencil'.

When choosing the vocabulary you intend teaching, here are some important things to consider.

Ten nouns – look for:
- High frequency, familiar words.
- Functional, useful words.
- Words that are related by topic.
- Words that feature clearly with good illustrations in the book.
- Words that also feature around the nursery in other contexts such as real objects, pictures, feature in other books.
- Words that you can support easily with visual resources such as toy objects, pictures, symbols, photos etc.

If you can identify less than 10 object words in the book which relate to your chosen topic, you can either just teach those seven or eight or choose additional related nouns to supplement those in the book, but make sure that you have visual resources with which to teach them. It is better to teach two or three related words that do not feature in the book than to choose two or three words which are pictured in the book but which do not relate to the theme.

Five verbs – look for:
- High frequency, familiar words.
- Functional, useful words.
- Verbs that relate to the nouns chosen, such as 'eating' and 'cooking' relate to food, 'wearing' and 'washing' relate to clothes.
- Verbs that are easy to act out. Think of an action for each verb and, if appropriate, a noise.

As with nouns, supplement the actions shown in the story with additional ones not featured, if they relate to the topic. For example, you have decided to choose the topic 'food'. The main verb featured is 'eating'. Other verbs that occur in the story are 'talking' and 'watching' but these are too abstract and do not relate to the topic of food. Instead choose verbs that are related to food and can be used in similar sentences, for example 'cooking' and 'cutting'. Then a sentence such as 'boy eating sausages' can easily be adapted to 'boy cooking sausages' or 'boy cutting sausages'. This gives children more sentence options while not changing other words in the sentence or the sentence structure, making it easier for them.

Two concepts – look for:

- High frequency, familiar words.
- Functional useful words.
- Concepts that relate to the nouns chosen.
- Those concepts most visually presented or most repeated in the story.
- A pair of concepts.
- Concepts that can be experienced practically around the nursery in a range of other activities.
- Where concepts are not necessarily in a pair, for example, positional words such as 'in', 'on', 'under', 'behind', 'in front' and 'next to', choose no more than three and start with the simplest, such as 'in', 'on', and 'under'.

For more able children who have a broad vocabulary and are competent users of the main object words featured in the story, you can still continue to expand their vocabularies in two different ways. Firstly you can teach them the relevant category name. For example, if you are working on clothes as a topic, explain to them that these things are all types of 'clothes'. Secondly, teach them parts of a whole vocabulary. For example, if you are teaching vehicles as a topic and are confident that the children know the object words 'car', 'bus', 'train', 'aeroplane' and so on, you can then begin to teach the words for their parts such as 'wheel', 'door', 'lights', 'bumper', 'engine', 'wing'. If we put all this together we can chart our plan for vocabulary as on the following page.

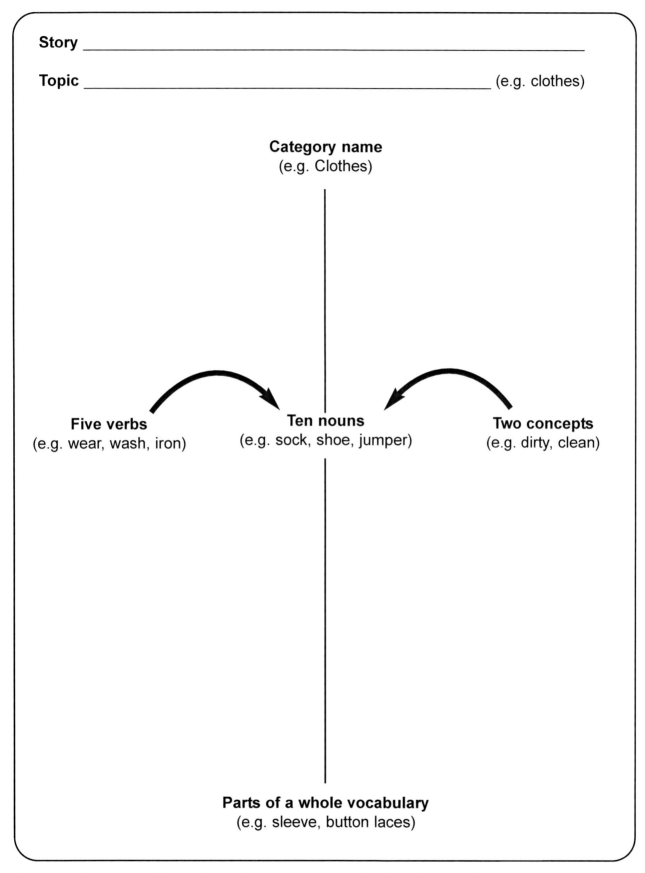

Story _____

Topic _____ (e.g. clothes)

Category name
(e.g. Clothes)

Five verbs
(e.g. wear, wash, iron)

Ten nouns
(e.g. sock, shoe, jumper)

Two concepts
(e.g. dirty, clean)

Parts of a whole vocabulary
(e.g. sleeve, button laces)

You can photocopy this and use it as a planning sheet, but remember:

- verbs and concepts *must* relate to the objects;
- category names and parts of a whole vocabulary *must* only be used with children who confidently know and use the 10 object words chosen.

Chapter 5   How do I keep this moving?
The next stages

In Chapter 4 we looked at developing a child's vocabulary of single words, the 'word bank', from which all sentences can be constructed. But clearly, building up a child's repertoire of words is not going to solve all their difficulties. Children with language delay and disorder also need help in knowing how to put those words together in combinations that build sentences that make sense. And later, these children will need help to order and string together combinations of complex ideas to recall some 'news' or a simple story.

Development of language skills as a basis for learning and literacy

The *Stories for Talking* approach is very structured and purposefully breaks down this learning into three stages to help the early years practitioner guide the children through this complex process of learning expressive language. Therefore, for each story there are three levels to work through:

- Level 1 – vocabulary building.
- Level 2 – sentence construction.
- Level 3 – sequencing and narrative.

Moving through and developing these skills is not only essential for development in speaking, but also provides the foundation for a lot of learning in the early years. A child relies heavily on listening, understanding and talking as a basis for learning in the early years. While play is the main vehicle of learning at this stage, this needs to be supplemented by the language needed to discuss, question, comment and share in their discoveries. Children learn so much through their own discoveries, experiences and thoughts with their peers and the adults in their learning environment. A language delayed or disordered child can be a very isolated learner.

Think of a group of normally developing children and a tuned in, responsive adult, playing in the water tray with fish and sea creatures. Do they not learn so much more than the names of the toys and the feel of the water, through each one sharing in their experiences of the seaside, rock pools, boat trips, and the adult responding by adding ideas and using new describing words to enrich those stories? Now think of the language delayed child and how much less they learn as they fail to understand most of what is said, fail to add their 'story' through lack of words, and, therefore, fail to get much of a response from the adult and peers around them. The learning experience is so much more limited.

And then, very soon, literacy is introduced and language, once again, is essential to a good start in learning to read and write. Before long the normally developing child is learning to create simple sentences to convey in writing, telling their 'news' or stating their preferences. Quickly they learn to put a few sentences together and the beginnings of narrative emerge. Sadly, children with language delay/disorder who have impoverished language skills as a basis on which to build literacy, are already at a big disadvantage. And as we all know, the curriculum becomes increasingly literacy-based as the main channel of learning.

The *Stories for Talking* approach aims to build those foundational skills at a pre-school age, before literacy becomes such an important part of the curriculum. The three levels of this approach provide a structured and graduated approach which aims to strengthen language skills as a foundation for **conversation** and **learning**; and strengthen language skills as a foundation for **literacy** but using spoken words instead of written words.

Level 1: vocabulary building

This level is aimed at those children who have very few words. Their repertoire of everyday vocabulary is limited and they need lots of help at learning new words introduced at nursery. The overall aim of this level is to develop vocabulary in the three areas of 'object', 'action' and 'concept' words.

Some children with severe difficulties may not be able to cope with the 'ten objects, five verbs and two concepts' approach outlined. For these children, limit the number of words introduced:

- teach object words before verbs and concepts;
- teach only four or five object words instead of 10;
- teach only the object words featured in the story (not the extra ones which may have been added to the selection featured in the book).

When teaching new words always use visual aids to help learning and retention of words. Use objects, pictures, actions, noises, real experiences, signs and symbols wherever possible. Use these visual resources throughout the nursery session, not just in the story session alone.

Introducing the vocabulary that will be taught in the story session before storytime, for example, through having toys available in nursery in free play, will help children learn new vocabulary.

Level 2: building sentences

This level is aimed at children who have a good grasp of basic vocabulary, but who use only single words or short phrases to communicate. They need help at learning how to combine these 'building blocks', i.e. using words, together in the right order to make sentences – first only short two word phrases and then longer sentences.

In each story section, you will find two options at Level 2 – 2a is to help children learn how to combine two words together in different combinations. For example:

- person/object and action word = 'cow eating', 'boy running'
- action word and object = 'eating cake', 'washing socks'.

In 2b, the aim is for children to build three word sentences, or sentences involving three ideas or components:

- The boy | is wearing | a hat
- The dog | is running | in the field

You will need to choose the level to work at depending on the language skills of the children in the group. If all the children in the group need help in building simple sentences, but some are more competent than others, it is better to teach at the level required by the less competent children. This way the more able children will have an opportunity to practise newly emerging skills and increase confidence, while the weaker children have an opportunity to learn new skills.

When introducing the *Stories for Talking* approach, begin teaching at the level the child is already at – use one week/story section to work at this level. This will build competence and confidence, and this will be useful time to practise social skills before going up a level to practise building longer sentences.

Consolidate new learning at the same level for a few weeks/story sections. For example, you have begun working at 2a 'putting two words together' through a story, and the children are beginning to grasp this skill. Next story, continue working at 2a, perhaps putting two words together in a different type of combination. *Do not* move on to 2b 'three words together' the next time – the children will need lots of practice with different vocabulary via different stories, and different combinations of words, to consolidate this skill of putting two words together before moving on.

Children with language difficulties require *lots* of repetition to help them learn. In some cases it may be useful, particularly with children with severe difficulties, to build phrases and sentences by varying only one word at a time. For example, if teaching two words together, it is easier for them to learn if they see/hear:
- '<u>eating</u> cake'
- '<u>eating</u> banana'
- '<u>eating</u> bread'
- '<u>eating</u> sausage'

before they hear:
- 'eating cake'
- 'drinking milk'
- 'wearing shorts'
- 'brushing teeth'

Similarly, a child learning to put three words together will find it easier if they hear/see:
- '<u>boy wearing</u> hat'
- '<u>boy wearing</u> shoes'
- '<u>boy wearing</u> jumper'

before they hear:
- 'boy wearing hat'
- 'girl wearing shoes'
- 'man wearing jumper'

Initially, when teaching new sentence structures:

- only vary one word at a time;
- keep the action word the same;
- use a limited number of object words to put together with the action word, to create variations in the sentence.

When teaching children how to put words together in phrases and sentences, only use vocabulary they already know and are confident with. If you know they struggle to remember the words for certain items, do not use these in sentence building work. Add other vocabulary as the child's sentence building skills improve.

Use the events pictured in the story to comment on when building sentences, before making up sentences from ideas in your/their thoughts. Use 'concrete', picture-based material before abstract ideas.

Use objects, or pictures of objects, wherever possible, to 'act out' the sentence as they are saying it. This helps them visualise the 'building blocks' they are trying to put together. For example, if trying to help children describe a teddy eating an apple, have a teddy and an apple available, so that the child can hold the objects and act out the sentence, as he/she builds the sentence. It is easier to see which 'bits' of the sentence you need when you are holding them/acting out with them, rather than trying to imagine it in your head. Using the child's visual channels in this way supports their thoughts, planning, word recall and sequencing of words in sentences.

As referred to earlier, two very useful strategies that adults should use in these structured story sessions (and generally in commentary in play) with the children are *modelling* and *expansion*.

With *modelling*, you model the kind of sentence you want the child to produce, using lots of repetition. For example, Joshua uses only single words, and your aim is for him to use two word phrases. You are playing in the sand with Joshua – you model:

digging	-	digging sand
bucket	-	big bucket
gone	-	sand gone
spade	-	Joshua's spade, Eva's spade

As he constantly hears models of two word phrases using words he already knows and uses in his talking, he is more likely to begin trying to put two words together himself.

With *expansion*, when a child speaks to you, you repeat what they have said and add another word on. For example:

Ruby: *bus*
You: *yes . . .* **big** *bus*
Ruby: *car*
You: *yes . . .* **blue** *car*

or

> Fred: *daddy gone*
> You: *daddy gone **work***
> Fred: *mummy shops*
> You: *mummy **gone** to shops*
> Fred: *mummy sweeties*
> You: *mummy's **buying** sweeties*

or

> Fatima: *boy eating sandwiches*
> You: *yes, boy eating a **cheese** sandwich*
> Fatima: *girl eating ice cream*
> You: *girl eating **cold** ice cream . . . yum yum*

As you can see, this strategy can be used at any stage, once the child has begun to speak some words. It is a very effective strategy, as it:

- allows space and time for the child to offer language;
- shows you have listened and acknowledged their comments;
- provides a model for them to learn to progress their sentence building skills on to the next level, by adding another word.

Both in free play and in structured sessions, you can be teaching sentence building skills purely by the way you respond to children in *your* talking. A setting where these strategies are in constant use becomes one of the most effective language and communication rich environments.

Level 3: Sequencing and narrative

Narrative (or telling a story) is a vastly more complex skill, and many children who may appear reasonably competent at language, with relatively good vocabulary and sentence building skills, may struggle at recalling or creating stories or retelling events.

As children get older, narrative (in the form of the written word) becomes a large part of the curriculum. However, even in the Early Years Foundation Stage (EYFS), narrative is very much a part of literacy in the Early Learning Goals. Clearly, we need to equip our language delayed learners as best we can before the learning demands of literacy descend upon them.

Narrative is also central to social development, which is very important to any pre-schooler, before literacy becomes relevant to them. A great deal of our relating to one another involves sound, narrative skills. In starting conversation with each other we spend a lot of time recounting events, telling news – it's a way in which people learn who we are, how we 'tick' – so it also plays a part in the development of our own self-identity.

Imagine a competent pre-schooler who can approach an adult, recall the details, sequence and outcome, of some special (or even mundane) event from the previous night, before happily going off to the home corner/role play area to engage in conversation, creating a 'story' of events there with their friends. Those abilities are dependent on a wide range, and combination, of skills. Narrative is highly complex and it is important to unpick some of the basic skills involved:

Content – A wide range of vocabulary is required to convey the detail of an event. Generally the story will require information on who is involved, what they are doing, where they are and why things happen. This requires words from across all the different word classes – objects, verbs, concepts and grammatical words.

Grammar – All those words need to be strung together in sentences, but narrative also requires more complex grammatical concepts such as 'so', 'then', 'next', 'because', 'when' and so on.

Sequencing – Those sentences then need to be put together in an order which makes sense, progressing through and connecting together the ideas and events. Sequencing skills depend on an understanding of time – moving on, from a beginning, to a middle, then an end.

Pragmatics – Awareness of the purpose of telling the story and an awareness of the listener is crucial. 'Losing the plot', going off at a tangent, giving too much detail – all these are traits that we can see in adults around us who have not quite mastered the art of storytelling. Their weak pragmatic skills mean we often switch off from our conversation with them or end up very confused. Children have to learn these subtle, yet crucial skills, as they develop their narrative skills.

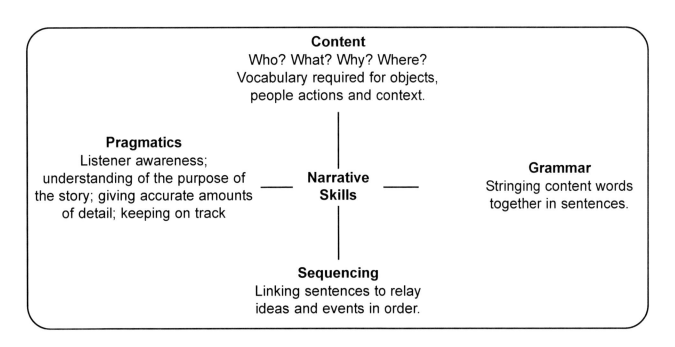

Clearly, with so many complex skills involved, children with language difficulties are especially likely to experience problems with narrative skills:

- Often, they do not develop grammatical words such as 'then', 'because', 'but', 'when', until much later than their peers.
- They lack understanding of the question words used to trigger awareness of the story components, for example 'who', 'where', 'how', 'why', 'what happened'.
- Narrative is highly reliant on the organisational skill of sequencing. This is frequently an inherent part of the difficulties experienced by children with language difficulties.
- Language is known to be a significant component in the development of our thinking and reasoning skills. Therefore, weak language skills will also weaken creativity in thinking and imagining.
- Children who have language difficulties frequently have difficulties with symbolic and imaginative play, which again are skills that underpin the early development of story-telling in a pre-school child.

Many narrative activities are too complex, and some programmes to develop narrative are very demanding for young children with severe language difficulties. This is the strength of the *Stories for Talking* approach. It provides a basic introduction to narrative. It takes simple and early steps to begin to develop some of the basic skills required, based on models of real and familiar stories the children hear repetitively for a week at storytime. It introduces the concept of sequencing, encourages recall of the basic defining events of a familiar story and encourages children to begin to explore linking sentences together, to create the basics of a 'story'.

Each story section, therefore, includes a daily programme of activities which need to be followed in order. For each story, the child initially engages in basic sequencing work starting at visually matching pictures to the story book, and later recalling the story using sequencing pictures. Later in the week, the child may be involved in making up very simple stories. The aim is not for them to be able to create wildly imaginative, detailed and flowing stories, but rather to give them the opportunity to experiment with creative storytelling and combining sentences and ideas. This will also enable them to:

- Develop their imagination, thinking outside of what is the concrete story in the book.
- Think sequentially – the fact that they make up a sentence following on from another child, rather than sentences in isolation.
- Generate new sentences with familiar vocabulary from the story.
- Learn how to link sentences together, how to identify a common theme, introducing the notion of making sense.

However, it is not the aim to have a story that 'makes sense' – if the children are creating sentences to put together in a 'story' it does not matter at this stage if it goes off at a tangent. Your role as the adult is to pull it back together with an ending that makes reasonable sense!

Visual aids such as toys and puppets are also involved in the activities described. It is much easier to envisage an event or story when the parts of the story are there to use to act out, rather than imagining an event in your head.

General approaches to developing narrative skills

In addition to the structured activities in the *Stories for Talking* approach there is, of course, lots that can be done throughout the nursery session to help encourage narrative skills.

- Talk about the concepts of 'beginning' and 'end'. These concepts are key in understanding how sequencing and stories work, so any chance to talk about these concepts will help develop awareness of sequence and time.

- Use question words from time to time throughout the child's play. Develop their play one step further by asking 'where are they going?', 'what will they do?', 'why did that happen?' and so on. (Remember to limit questions in your interaction with language delayed and disordered children. Only use these questions to evoke narrative and story telling with children who have competent basic language skills and are able to readily build sentences and engage in conversation.)

- Encourage pretend play. Some children tend to be 'on the edge' – they want to join in but are not sure how to get involved in the story. You can help greatly by giving them a role. For example:

  'Sam, you're playing a great shopping game, but I think there's another customer waiting here! James, do you need to buy something at this shop?' Encourage James, and help him to get the right 'gear', such as a basket, and help him think about what to ask for, like, 'apples and bananas, please'.

- Similarly, if a competent child is telling you about an event that has happened, for example, his trip to the park last night, and there is a quiet child standing by, help them to join in. For example:

  'That's great Tom that you went on that big slide' (Turn to Emma) 'Do you like to go to the slides Emma?'

  Encourage quieter less confident/competent children to join in with little conversations, using the more able children's talk as a good model and draft for discussion.

- Develop children's imaginative play and consequently their storytelling. You could either model new ideas to develop what they are already doing, or offer questions/choices to lead them into a new idea. For example:

  Mark is playing with the small world playground. He is enjoying putting a boy down a slide repetitively but does not show any other pretend/imaginative skills. You could say: 'I've got a little girl here – she likes the roundabout. She's shouting 'hey boy, do you want to come and play with me on this roundabout?' And later, 'Here's her mum coming now. Do you think her mum will go on a swing or sit on this bench?'

On the surface this may appear to be simple play, but these imaginative thoughts and sequences of new ideas are as crucial to storytelling as the words and sentences themselves, and do in fact support and develop the language skills required. Take time to recall everyday sequences in nursery. You can do this by:

- talking through the plan for the day – what is going to happen/what has happened;

- talking through and recalling a special activity such as baking or a creative activity. Talk about it in order using words and concepts such as 'first', 'then', 'next', 'at the end' and so on. This develops those crucial sequencing and recall skills;

- using puppet play to encourage story telling;

- having story sack toy material out to play with to enable children to recall familiar stories with the objects and book in front of them. Allow them space to play with these without an adult to have lots of freedom to make up new stories and events with the familiar characters.

Development of social interaction skills as a basis for relationships

People are social beings. People need relationships, and relationships need communication. In addition to language, communication and social interaction are also based on other skills, many non-verbal such as eye contact, facial expression, smiles and laughs, pointing, gesture and body language. Even a child with little or no language can communicate in some way if they are motivated and socially 'tuned in' to relate to others. We see this babies, who can be highly competent at engaging us long before they have words and sentences.

However, a great deal of social development, particularly by the age of three, is based on language-orientated interaction. A pre-schooler with competent age-appropriate language and skills is able to request, comment, engage in basic negotiation, share news, take turns in early conversation, share ideas, problem solve and discuss outcomes of an event.

A language-disordered or delayed child, therefore, is at a major disadvantage in terms of the effect this has on social skills and development. In addition to a difficulty with learning language, these children tend to have inherent difficulties with attention and listening skills, affecting their ability to listen to others, and take turns, both in conversation and while playing.

There are also many secondary effects of difficulties with language that impact on a child's social development. These children tend to be less confident in using their language for a range of different purposes, for example, requesting, directing, commenting, sharing information and suggesting ideas. They are generally less able to join in with group games, often left playing on the edge if not entirely excluded. Consequently, issues of low self-esteem develop early on in childhood, with poor social confidence leading to a passive and isolated child. On other occasions, children can develop negative, aggressive behaviour difficulties, an inability to negotiate, discuss or even make a simple verbal request leading to snatching or hitting. The child becomes known by his/her peers as aggressive and tends to be feared and avoided, leading to isolation.

It is so important, therefore, that we do all we can as early years practitioners to help avoid this negative cycle by supporting and fostering social relationships in these vulnerable children. The *Stories for Talking* approach specifically aims to target social skills as part of the activities presented. Each session attempts to teach social skills and nurture relationships by providing:

- group activities rather than one-to-one programmes;
- small groups of the same children repeatedly, to boost confidence and help children develop friendships with specific individuals;
- interaction and chat – child:adult and child:child are encouraged;

- Specific activities provide structured and supported opportunities to use language with their peers, specifically addressing skills of
  - listening to others;
  - taking turns;
  - making requests;
  - asking questions;
  - directing others using messages/instructions.

So in addition to those who have language difficulties, children who are shy or withdrawn, or who tend to be isolated learners, will also benefit from this programme.

Some children who have severe social interaction difficulties which are part of the autistic spectrum may gain something from this approach, but are likely to require very high levels of support. It is advisable to consult professionals involved with these children as to the suitability of this programme for such children.

Early Learning Goals covered by *Stories for Talking*
(as laid out in *The Early Years Foundation Stage* (DCFS, 2008)

Communication, Language and Literacy
- Interact with others, negotiating plans and activities and taking turns in conversation.
- Extend their vocabulary, exploring the meanings and sounds of new words.
- Speak clearly and audibly with confidence and control, and show awareness of the listener.
- Use language to imagine and recreate roles and experiences.
- Use talk to organise, sequence and clarify thinking, ideas, feelings and events.
- Explore and experiment with sounds, words and texts.
- Retell narratives in the correct sequence, drawing on language patterns of stories.
- Show an understanding of the elements of stories, such as main character, sequence of events.

Personal, Social and Emotional Development
- Be confident to try new activities, initiate ideas and speak in a familiar group.
- Maintain attention, concentrate and sit quietly when appropriate.
- Form good relationships with adults and peers.
- Work as part of a group or class, taking turns and sharing fairly.

Creative Development
- Use their imagination in art, design, music, dance, imaginative and role play and stories.
- 'Express and communicate their ideas, thoughts and feelings by using a widening range of materials, suitable tools, imaginative and role play, movement, designing and making, and a variety of songs and musical instruments.

Problem Solving, Reasoning and Numeracy
- Use everyday words to describe position.

Knowledge and Understanding of the World
- Find out about their environment, and talk about those features they like and dislike.
- Ask questions about why things happen and how things work.

Chapter 6   Sharing this with others – involving carers in the progress

The child's parents/carers are so important in the development of any child's language skills. This programme is not intended as a parent-skilling package, but does seek to actively involve the parent/carer in the learning process. It is really important to keep the carers informed, but better still to involve them and give them a role. We want to take the confidence, self-esteem and enjoyment that children begin to experience into other settings rather than restricting it to just their time at pre-school.

So each level for each story has a concrete, structured and relevant activity for the children to take home to share. The aim is to **build confidence** – not only in the child, but also in parents/carers. It is not to be seen as 'homework', but fun to be shared, so we need to make sure that the activity is straightforward and easy for the child and carer to achieve.

The programme also provides a foundation from which they can begin to develop their child's language in other related ways. It may be as simple as them using the target vocabulary (i.e. the topic the activity is based on, such as 'clothes' or 'food') in general conversation. This encourages the child's broader understanding of the meaning of the words as well as giving them opportunities to learn to use them functionally. Imagine how empowered a child would feel if he was able to use the new 'food' words he had learned in nursery, to ask for his favourite snack or tell his mum what he wanted for dinner.

Hopefully, doing a story-based activity at home might encourage parents/carers to seek out other books with those words and pictures in, or possibly find relevant toys or games. All are excellent triggers for conversation and building of social skills and relationships. Being involved in this way may turn a shopping trip from a real chore into a positive learning experience – or perhaps inspire a special day out for the family, such as to a local farm.

Encourage the *whole* family to get involved. Often the activity is a game so mums, dads, siblings, grandparents, neighbours – everyone could be involved. This will help to raise the child's confidence and use of language with a wider range of people. It also means that more people involved with the child are 'clued in' to provide helpful and relevant comments and conversations. Language difficulties often run in families, so we may also be helping any other siblings at the same time.

Finally, another reason why we should involve parents/carers is because repetition leads to retention. The more we repeat new words, sentences and stories, the more likely children will become familiar with them and remember them.

Some practical aspects to consider
1) Try and allow 10-15 minutes at the end of a session at the end of the week to tell parents/carers about the:
    a) story covered – brief details will do;
    b) target language you've been working on e.g., the new vocabulary words, or the sentence building skills;
    c) parent/carer activity – show and demonstrate, as well as explain.

You may think that the game is really obvious and only needs a little explanation, but some parents/carers may not be familiar with the format, so always go through it. It is always a good idea to demonstrate – all of us learn better from seeing as well as listening, and especially parents/carers with language difficulties themselves will need you to show them what to do.

It is really important to stress at the end of each session with the parents/carers that the activity is to build confidence, that it is *not* homework, and it should always involve praise and positive comments.

2) Explain to the children in their storytime that this is the game they can take home to do with their family members. Always demonstrate it to the children too. You may be more skilled at showing and explaining than their parents/carers, and this prior knowledge will support the child's confidence and will therefore make for a more successful outcome to the activity.

3) The parent/carer activity resources should always be given, not loaned. Then you have no worries as to whether they will ever be seen again, and the parents/carers do not have to worry if the child spills juice all over them or they get eaten by the dog! For this reason all the resources in this book are photocopiable.

4) If possible, loan the story book to the parents/carers. Better still, get your creative parents/carers to make some storysacks. Storysacks are fantastic resources (for more details have a look at www.storysacks.co.uk). They are designed to be shared with parents/carers and have lovely practical objects to make the stories come alive. Adults love them as much as children.

5) Each week, at the beginning of a new story, have a little display in the area where the parents/carers wait, or at least pass by. All it needs is:
    a)   a poster of the story featured this week and the topic covered;
    b)   a copy of the book for parents/carers to glance through as they wait.

6) You could possibly have a session such as a coffee morning, for the parents/carers at the beginning of their child's time in nursery. These groups could be used to:
    a)   explain what *Stories for Talking* will be like, and how the rest of the curriculum activities will be linked to it;
    b)   explain their role and the parent/carer activity;
    c)   encourage them to visit the local library and borrow the same, or other, relevant stories. You could arrange for your local librarian to come in and introduce themselves;
    d)   mention and encourage storysacks;
    e)   if you have one, show a video of other *Stories for Talking* groups (remember, you will need written parental permission from the parents/carers of the children filmed).

Try and think of other ways of getting parents/carers involved. No matter what the parents/carers of the children you work with are like and whatever circumstances they are in, once involved they will all do something – be it a tiny change or a highly enthusiastic response, which makes it all worthwhile.

Chapter 7   Measuring progress – record keeping

The *Stories for Talking* approach is ideally suited to provide evidence for your continuous assessment, setting and meeting targets for individual children, and monitoring a child's progress in the area of Communication, Language and Literacy.

While this approach is based on small group sessions, it can easily be differentiated so that individual children's targets can be set within the group.

It is both highly structured (concrete activities in the story session for the early years practitioner to implement) and yet can also be used flexibly. The evidence gained from observation and basic recording of language samples provides a wealth of information for baseline assessment, without creating yet more paperwork for the early years practitioner.

Planning your assessment

1. Perform a pre-story screen
- Spend five to ten minutes with each child on a one-to-one basis, looking through the book to be covered in the *Stories for Talking* sessions.
- Do not read the story – just look through the book with the child, saying something like: 'Let's see what's happening in these pictures'.
- Give the child plenty of time to volunteer any language to describe the pictures. Write down any single words or sentences used to describe the pictures.
- If the child is silent or simply points, respond with comments like: 'Oh look! A cat'. Does the child attempt to imitate you? Also, see if the child can point to any pictures on request. For example: 'Can you show me the banana?' Write down any words understood or copied.

This information will be very important in determining at which level you need to run your *Stories for Talking* group – at single word/no vocabulary level, (Level 1), at phrase/sentence building level (Level 2) or at narrative/story telling level (Level 3). It also provides a basis from which progress can be monitored.

2. Follow-up with a post-story review
- This can be used to review any targets set for individual children (see Individual Education Plans below) or simply to monitor the effectiveness of the *Stories for Talking* programme.
- Do not review the children straight after the sessions on that book (wait a few weeks after the pre-story screen). Children require time for consolidating the skills they learn. Ongoing learning of vocabulary, sentences and storytelling will continue through play for many weeks after a particular story has finished.
- Review the child's progress after half or a whole term. Once again, look through the books you have covered on a one-to-one basis, letting the child lead the discussion.

- Let the child choose the books, pages etc, s/he wants to start with. Let the child initiate the talk, at their level.
- Make notes of the language used (or a sample of it if there is a lot), and comment on their sequencing and story telling ability, if this is appropriate.

You may find it useful to use the vocabulary planning sheet on page 21 for each topic/book, as a checklist for vocabulary. You will need one sheet per child. Use the sheet to mark the words labelled at both pre-screen and post-review. Also write down any phrases or sentences used on the back of the sheet. These sheets can be kept in individual children's records as evidence of progress and any area of difficulty.

Target Setting and Individual Education Plans (IEPs)

Target setting can be as simple as assigning a child to a *Stories for Talking* programme and deciding at which level the group will run.

The *Special Educational Needs Code of Practice* (DfES, 2001) states that children who have been identified as having SEN and who are at the 'Early Years Action' stage, should be supported via individualised arrangements for learning and teaching. Participation in *Stories for Talking* at an appropriate level would be an effective form of support for children at this stage.

Where a child is experiencing significant difficulties and interventions planned through Early Years Action have not resulted in the child making sufficient progress, the 'Early Years Action Plus' stage of the Code of Practice will apply. These children are likely to have external support agencies involved, for example, speech and language therapy or early years support services. These children will require more specific written targets which can be documented on their IEP. Where external agencies are involved with a child, it is very important that you discuss the targets set as part of the *Stories for Talking* programme to ensure they are at the appropriate level.

Targets set as part of the programme need to be individual to the child, specific and measurable. Targets covering a range of difficulties can be met via this programme. A list of positive targets that could be set may include:
- Ellie to show understanding of 20 new object words.
- Derris to label 20 new object words.
- George to label 10 new verb words.
- Mohammed to show understanding of 4 new concept words.
- Anne to combine 2 words in short sentences
    - in response to picture material,
    - in spontaneous language.
- Jordan to attend to a group for 10 minutes, in a small group situation.
- Brandon to show increased confidence in social situations by volunteering single words in a small group setting.
- Shrishti to show increased awareness of others by taking turns in a small group activity.
- Joseph to sequence 3 pictures relating to a familiar story.

- Priya to retell 4 key aspects of a story.
- Dominic to use language in spontaneous conversation in a familiar play situation.
- Elizabeth to take part in familiar role play
  - being aware of others and taking a role,
  - using language appropriately as part of a role.

Individual Education Plans also need to specify review dates and outcomes (see following page for an example IEP that could be written for a child taking part in a *Stories for Talking* programme).

In addition to the post-story review, any samples of language used in functional, social and play settings should be used as evidence of progress to monitor and review targets. This approach gives the early years practitioner both the focus and time to observe the child's spontaneous language skills, in addition to the information provided by the pre-story screen and post-story review. This information can be used in developmental profiles such as baseline assessments.

Sample Individual Education Plan

Name: Ben Potts **Date: 27 January 2008** **Review Date: March 2008**

Aim	Objective	How	Who	When	Measurable Target	Target Achieved Y/N
To improve Ben's comprehension of language	Ben to understand 2 key word instructions	Comprehension activities in *Stories for Talking*	Storytime group leader	Storytime group	Follows 80% of 2 key word instructions	
To improve Ben's expressive language	Ben to learn new verb vocabulary	• Expressive activities for verbs in *Stories for Talking* • Modelling of verbs by staff in play	• Storytime group leader • All staff	• Storytime session • Free play sessions	Ben to label 10 new verb words	
To improve Ben's confidence in using language	Ben to use language in a small group setting	Encourage contributions in all activities in *Stories for Talking*	Storytime group leader	Storytime group	Ben to use single words 5 times in a small group session	
To extend Ben's attention span	Ben to attend in a small group setting	Focus attention and encourage participation in interactive small groups	Storytime group leader	Storytime group	Ben to attend to group activity for 10 minutes	

Stories for Talking programme

Dora's Eggs

by Julie Sykes and Jane Chapman

Section index

Dora's Eggs

Section index continued

		Page
Level 3	**Narrative**	50
Weekly plan		
Monday	Sequencing – matching pictures	50
Tuesday	Sequencing – using memory	50
Wednesday	Retelling the story with toys	50
Thursday	Creating a new story	51
Friday	Creating a new story	51
Parent/carer activity		51
Generalising language and skills within the EYFS		52

Dora's Eggs

Level 1 – Introducing vocabulary

Topic category	Animals (farm animals)	
Nouns (object words) – basic level	**hen** **egg** **duck** **pig** **sheep** **dog** **cow** **cat** **horse** **mouse**	
Notes	Whilst 'egg' is not a farm animal, it has been included in the list of basic object vocabulary as it is so central to the story and appears in the title of the book. The first seven words chosen appear in the book. 'Cat', 'horse', and 'mouse' do not feature in the book and have been added to complete the set of ten object words as they are other well known farm animals. If appropriate, substitute other basic farm animal words of your own choice instead of these three.	
Verbs (action words)	**sitting** **swimming** **walking** **sleeping** **crying**	
Notes	This book mentions many other action words, but these five were chosen as they are the most concrete and are 'everyday' verbs (for example, 'playing' features in the story but this is a very general and vague verb and a pig or lamb playing is very different to the idea that children have about playing).	
Concepts	**happy** **sad**	
Notes	These concepts are central to the theme of the book, are seen every day, are functional and relate to the verb 'crying'.	
Parts of a whole vocabulary	**baby animals** **animal homes**	
Notes	Remember, this is only taught to children who have a good grasp of the basic vocabulary and are able to both understand and label (say) the basic words listed earlier. In this story 'baby animals' and 'animal homes' are used as the harder vocabulary rather than 'parts of animals' as this relates to the story much better.	
Harder nouns (object words)	**chick** **duckling** **calf** **puppy** **piglet** **lamb**	**nest** **pond** **cowshed** **field**

Story: Dora's Eggs

Topic: Farm animals

Farm animals

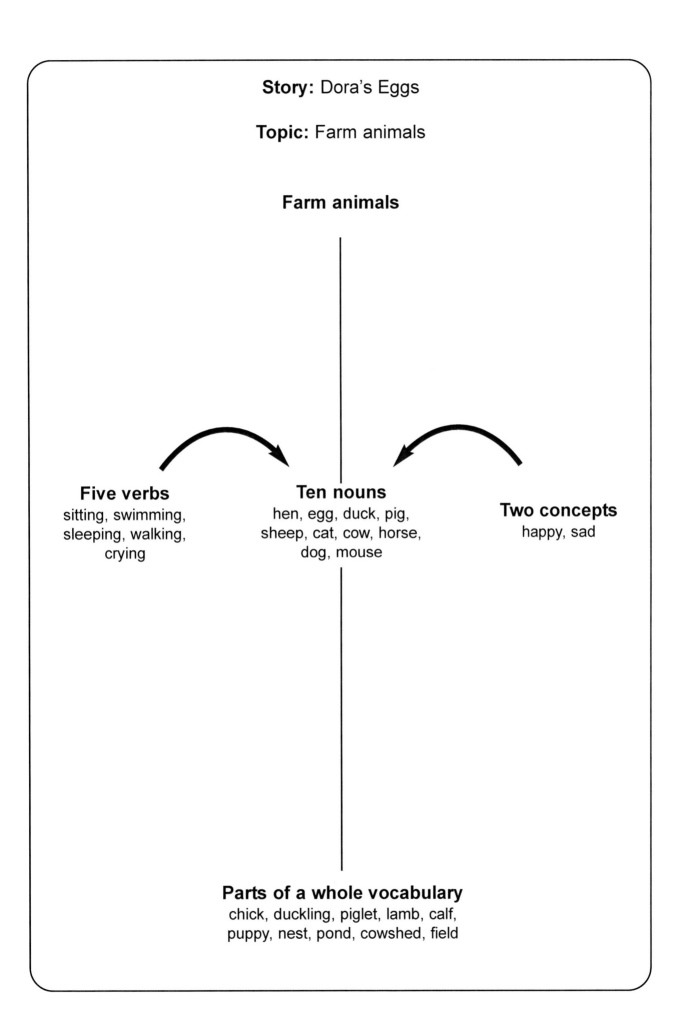

Five verbs
sitting, swimming,
sleeping, walking,
crying

Ten nouns
hen, egg, duck, pig,
sheep, cat, cow, horse,
dog, mouse

Two concepts
happy, sad

Parts of a whole vocabulary
chick, duckling, piglet, lamb, calf,
puppy, nest, pond, cowshed, field

Weekly plan for Level 1 – Introducing vocabulary	*Dora's Eggs*
Monday	
Focus	**Understanding object words**
What you need	Plastic farm animals to match the ten chosen object words. (If you are teaching the harder level vocabulary and are struggling to find toy objects, then use some pictures or photos. Ideally, try to make something which looks like a nest, field and so on.)
Activity 1	As you read the story, get the children to have a turn at finding the object and matching it to the picture in the book. You make a point of saying the name of the animal lots of times and if you know how to, sign it too.
Activity 2	Lay out the animals on the floor and ask each child in turn to find one. For example, 'Anna, find the pig', 'George, find the dog'.
Notes	Remember, each day when you read the story you will be pointing out and emphasising all of the key vocabulary as it appears in the story and pictures. All of the vocabulary is therefore mentioned each day, but on certain days the activities and resources you use will particularly focus on one of the different word classes.
Tuesday	
Focus	**Naming object words**
What you need	Objects (as above). A 'feely' bag (an interesting bag preferably with a drawstring top).
Activity 1	Pass the feely bag around the group. Each child has a turn to reach inside the bag, pull out an animal and try to name it.
Activity 2	Read the story – pause and leave a gap for children to name the animal as it appears in the story.
Wednesday	
Focus	**Understanding verbs (action words)**
What you need	'Feely' bag and objects as required on Tuesday.
Activity 1	Read the story. As you come across each of the chosen five verbs in the story, act them out and get the group to copy you.
Activity 2	Pass the feely bag around the group. Today they must take turns to get an animal out of the bag, name it, then listen to you. You must tell them what to make their animal do. For example: 'Oh, you've got the sheep John! Can you make it *walk*?'

Thursday	
Focus	**Naming verbs (action words)**
What you need	Verb cards (photocopy pages 57-59). Egg cards (photocopy page 60 and cut out).
Activity 1	Read the story. Use the verb cards and match them to the verbs as they are mentioned and pictured in the story. Stress the action word as you are doing it.
Activity 2	Use the verb cards to play a game 'Hunt the Egg'. Lay the verb cards face down on the floor; hide an egg under some of the pictures; each child must have a turn at choosing and turning over a verb card, naming the verb, acting out that verb, and also seeing if they have been lucky and won an egg. When they have named the verb, you can expand it into a two word phrase for them. For example: 'Yes Fred, it's 'sleeping' . . . 'duck sleeping'.' (Remember the 'expanding' strategy talked about in Chapter 2).
Friday	
Focus	**Understanding and naming concepts**
What you need	'Happy' and 'sad' cards (photocopy page 61 and cut out). Photographs of happy and sad people.
Activity 1	Give each child a 'happy' card and a 'sad' card. Act out with the group, being happy and being sad.
Activity 2	Look at the photographs. Get each child to take turns at looking at a photograph, deciding if the person is happy or sad and showing their happy or sad card. They may be able to use the correct concept word to tell you as well.
Activity 3	Read the story. Pause at each different animal and get the whole group to hold up their happy or sad cards and say which one the animal is feeling. You can then model a two word phrase, for example: 'Yes she's happy . . . pig's happy', 'oh dear, she's sad . . . hen's sad'. (Remember the modelling strategy in Chapter 2).
Parent/carer activity	Hunt the Egg game (as played on Thursday). You will need a copy of the verb cards and eggs for each child to take home (photocopy pages 57-60).

Weekly plan for Level 2a – Building phrases and sentences – two words together

Dora's Eggs

Monday	
Focus	**Modelling two word phrases**
What you need	Plastic farm animals (hen, sheep, dog, cow, duck, pig). Verb cards (photocopy pages 57-59). You will only need the ones which match the pictures in the book – hen sitting, duck swimming, dog walking, cow sleeping, hen crying. There are no pictures for the pig and the sheep.
Activity 1	Read the story. As you come to each page act out the different actions shown in the story with your toy animals, commenting on what you're doing using a two word phrase, for example: 'Look, dog walking'.
Activity 2	Go through the book again and match the verb cards to the picture in the story. Again, model the two word phrase as you do so.
Tuesday	
Focus	**Two key word comprehension**
What you need	Verb cards (all) – as photocopied for Monday.
Activity 1	Lay out all of the verb cards face up on the floor in front of all of the children. Ask individual children to find you a certain card, for example: 'Kyle, find the dog swimming'. When they find the card do not remove it – make sure all of the cards are present for each instruction given (otherwise the activity becomes easier as cards are removed and no longer tests the child at a two key word level).
Activity 2	Read the story, matching the picture cards to each page. You model the two word phrase (as you did yesterday).
Wednesday	
Focus	**Two key word comprehension**
What you need	Plastic farm animals.
Activity 1	Read the story, acting out each of the actions on each page with the toy animals. Model the two word phrase (just as you did on Monday).
Activity 2	Place the toy animals in front of the children. Give each child a little instruction, such as: 'Ella, make the duck sleep'; 'David, make the sheep walk'.

Weekly plan for Level 2a (continued)	*Dora's Eggs*
Thursday	
Focus	**Expressive language activity**
What you need	Plastic farm animals; verb cards.
Activity 1	Read the story, making the toy animals do the actions and modelling two word phrases.
Activity 2	Choose a child who will be assigned to the role of 'teacher' and ask them to choose a friend. The 'teacher' will give their friend a message to act out using the toys. The 'teacher' picks a verb card and then tells their friend what is on it, for example, 'cow sleeping'. The friend then carries this out with the toy animals. Both the 'teacher' and the friend will need support from you. Also the 'teacher' may need help to construct the sentence and the friend will need prompting to listen and may need you to repeat it again for them. Take it in turns so that each child has a chance to be both a 'teacher' and a 'friend'.
Friday	
Focus	**Expressive language activity**
What you need	Plastic farm animals; verb cards.
Activity 1	Repeat the activity from Thursday. Hopefully, the children will require less prompting and support from you.
Parent/carer activity	**Pairs:** Photocopy the verb cards (pages 57-59) twice for each child. Get parents/carers to cut up the cards and lay them face down. The players take turns to turn over and describe two cards. If they are the same they get to keep them, but if they are different (e.g. duck swimming . . . dog walking) they have to turn them back over. The winner is the one with the greatest number of pairs at the end.

Weekly plan for Level 2b – Building phrases and sentences – three words together	*Dora's Eggs*
Notes	These activities are for children who usually use short two or three word phrases and have a good vocabulary for basic objects. For this set of activities you will need to introduce more vocabulary than that shown on the vocabulary planner. You will introduce the vocabulary of 'animal homes': nest; henhouse; pond; shed; field.
Monday	
Focus	**Introducing vocabulary for sentence building**
What you need	Objects that represent animal homes (such as nest, henhouse, pond, shed and field; toy plastic animals; a feely bag (an interesting bag, preferably with a drawstring top).
Activity 1	Read the story.
Activity 2	Introduce 'animal homes' vocabulary. Have objects to represent each one. These can be simple, such as a sheet of blue plastic paper to represent the pond. Make sure that you show the picture in the book at the same time as the object so that the children make the connection between the two.
Activity 3	Put the plastic animals in the feely bag. Pass the bag around the children and let them take turns to get an animal and match it to the correct home. Use the book to check whether the child is right if they are unsure or get it wrong.
Tuesday	
Focus	**Two key word comprehension**
What you need	Animal homes; plastic animals.
Activity 1	Read the story.
Activity 2	Lay out the animals and homes. Give each child an instruction, for example: 'put the sheep in the pond'; 'put the hen in the shed'; 'put the pig in the henhouse'. You can make this into a 'silly' game, by saying things like: 'Oh! Is that right? I forgot! Where should the sheep go?' and so on. Don't ask the child to put the animal in its usual home, for example the hen in the henhouse. Instead they only need to understand the 'animal' and then would be able to deduce where it needs to go, rather than needing to listen for the part of the instruction relating to place.

Weekly plan for Level 2b (continued)	*Dora's Eggs*
Wednesday	
Focus	**Expressive language – building three word sentences**
What you need	Verb cards (photocopy pages 57-59); animal homes, plastic animals.
Activity 1	Read the story, highlighting the action and animal home, for example: 'Look at the cow! She's sleeping . . . here's her shed'. Then model a sentence: 'cow's sleeping' . . . 'the cow's sleeping in the shed'.
Activity 2	Use the verb cards. Each child takes it in turn to take a card and describes the picture on it, e.g. 'Sheep's eating'. Then the child gets that toy animal and decides where they want to put it, such as 'in the field'. Once they have put their animal in its place, encourage them to describe the scene. For example: 'The sheep's eating in the field'.
Thursday	
Focus	**Expressive language – giving messages – three word sentences**
What you need	Animal masks (photocopy pages 64-71); large animal homes props such as blue and green paper or plastic for the pond and field, a large box or material for the cowshed, a small box for the henhouse; verb cards (as Wednesday).
Activity 1	Read the story.
Activity 2	Use the masks, large 'homes' and verb cards to do some 'acting'. Choose a child who will be the 'teacher' who then picks up the verb card and decides where the animal should do the action. For example: 'Dog sitting . . . in the field'; 'hen crying . . . in the shed'. The 'teacher' then chooses another child and gives them the instruction. For example: 'The dog sitting in the field'. The other child has to find the right mask, put it on, and then act out the instruction in the correct animal home (they may need some help finding the right mask and putting it on).
Friday	
Focus	**Expressive language – giving messages**
What you need	As Thursday.
Activity 1	Read the story.
Activity 2	Repeat Thursday's activity, but with less prompts to the children. Then demonstrate the parent/carer activity.
Parent/carer activity	Use the 'baseboard' with animal homes (photocopy and enlarge page 56); cut out and stick the pictures of animals (photocopy pages 54-55) in their homes and get the children to describe the scene. For example: 'The hen's sitting on the nest'.

Weekly plan for Level 3 – Narrative	*Dora's Eggs*
Notes	The aim of this level is to give children an opportunity to experiment with creative story telling, develop combinations of two, three or more sentences, and develop an understanding and use of sequencing. Clearly, it is not suitable for children who have only recently begun to combine words in sentences.
Monday	
Focus	**Sequencing – matching pictures**
What you need	Sequencing pictures (photocopy pages 62-63).
Activity 1	Read the story.
Activity 2	Go back through the story and match the sequencing pictures to the corresponding part of the story. This will enable the children to lay out the sequencing cards in order.
Activity 3	Re-tell the story (in brief) from the sequencing strip of pictures.
Tuesday	
Focus	**Sequencing – using memory**
What you need	Sequencing pictures (as on Monday).
Activity 1	Read the story.
Activity 2	Without using the book, see if the children can sequence the pictures in order.
Activity 3	Re-tell the story from the sequencing strip.
Wednesday	
Focus	**Retelling the story with toys**
What you need	Sequencing pictures; toy farm animals.
Activity 1	Read the story.
Activity 2	Sequence the pictures.
Activity 3	Use the toys to act out and re-tell the story. Give each child one of the animals, including 'Dora' and encourage them to re-enact the story with the animals. Use the sequencing pictures to prompt if a child has difficulty.

Thursday	
Focus	**Creating a new story**
What you need	Photocopy pages 64-71 to make masks with elastic.
Activity 1	Read the story.
Activity 2	Model how to create a different story, making sure you tell the children what you're doing: 'I'm going to tell a different story about Dora and the animals'. For example: 'Dora has some eggs. She goes round to all the animals on the farm and invites them to come to a party for a surprise. She has some chicks and they all celebrate'. The children wearing animal masks are directed as you tell the story, to act it out.
Friday	
Focus	**Creating a new story**
What you need	Toy animals; other farm objects such as a tractor, shed, field, food and so on.
Activity 1	**Don't** read the story! You and the children will create your own story this time.
Activity 2	Start the story off. Each child has a turn to take a toy and try to tell a small part of the story. Make sure that you connect each part of the story and give it an ending. Do not worry if the children go off at a tangent, become repetitive, don't make logical suggestions or make up an exciting story. Initially, it is just about the children having an opportunity to be creative, expressing basic ideas and learning to take turns at being the storyteller.
Parent/carer activity	Photocopy the sequencing pictures for Dora's Eggs on pages 62-63 and send this home for them to practise sequencing and telling the story. If the children have made 'stick puppets' of the animals in the creative area of nursery, allow them to take these home to encourage simple conversation and story creation.

Dora's Eggs – generalising language and skills within the EYFS

Notes	Generalising the language and skills taught throughout other activities in the EYFS gives essential opportunities for **repetition** and **functional** use of language to improve social skills and confidence. Here are some examples of activities to build on the language of Dora's Eggs. Under each activity heading are just some possible Focuses of Development within the Early Years Foundation Stage.
Small world play/sand Knowledge and Understanding of the World – Place	Put toy animal figures and their babies in the sand together with different sized boxes to represent animal homes, and small sticks to build nests.
Role play, outdoors, construction (large building blocks) Problem Solving, Reasoning and Numeracy – Shape, Space and Measures	Using animal masks (photocopy pages 64-71) for children to wear, either use your outdoor equipment or use large cardboard boxes to make animal homes, a large blue plastic sheet/mat for a pond, grass and playground for the rest and encourage children to act out the story in their masks. Alternatively, encourage children to build homes for the animals using large construction blocks and then play in them with masks on.
Painting Knowledge and Understanding of the World – Designing and Making	Paint eggs – later you could have egg rolling races. Roll boiled eggs in paint and then on paper to make patterns (use a large plastic tray and tip it to roll the paint covered egg around, making a pattern).
Drawing Creative Development – Exploring Media and Materials	Have photographs and toy animals to encourage representational drawing.
Jigsaws Problem Solving, Reasoning and Numeracy – Shape, Space and Measures	Animal jigsaws.
Puppet theatre Creative Development – Developing Imagination and Imaginative Play	Make 'stick puppets' of farm animals (photocopy page 54-55) – stick them on to lollipop sticks to encourage story telling. You could even create a puppet theatre.
Baking Communication, Language and Literacy – Language for Thinking	Boil eggs and help the children make their own egg sandwiches for snack time. Make chocolate crispy nests with mini-eggs.
Listening games Communication, Language and Literacy – Language for Communication	Tapes of animal sounds. Try to make up your own tape with only the five animals featured on it (not those available commercially with loads of animals including dolphins and parrots).
Books Communication, Language and Literacy – Reading	Look for other stories and non-fiction books featuring farm animals. You can also make story sacks with farm animals.
Trips Knowledge and Understanding of the World – Place	Organise a trip to a farm or ask a local farmer to bring in some baby chicks.

Photocopiable Resources for *Dora's Eggs*

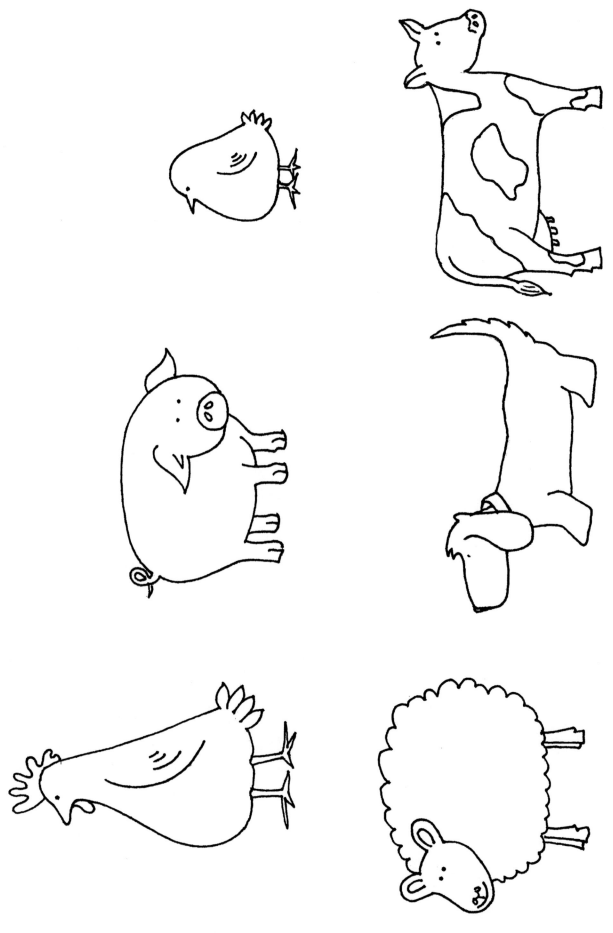

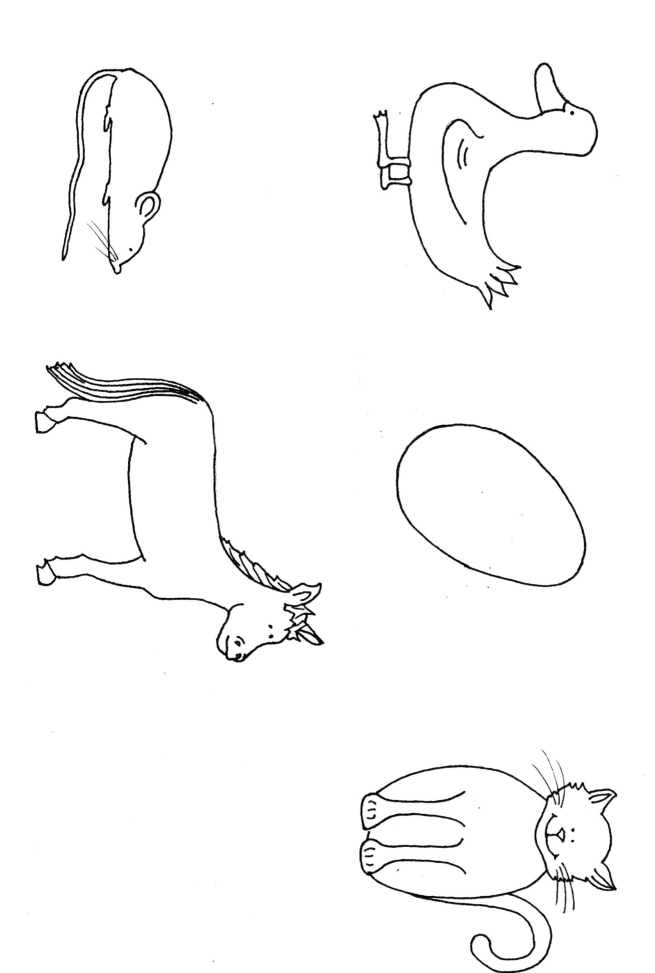

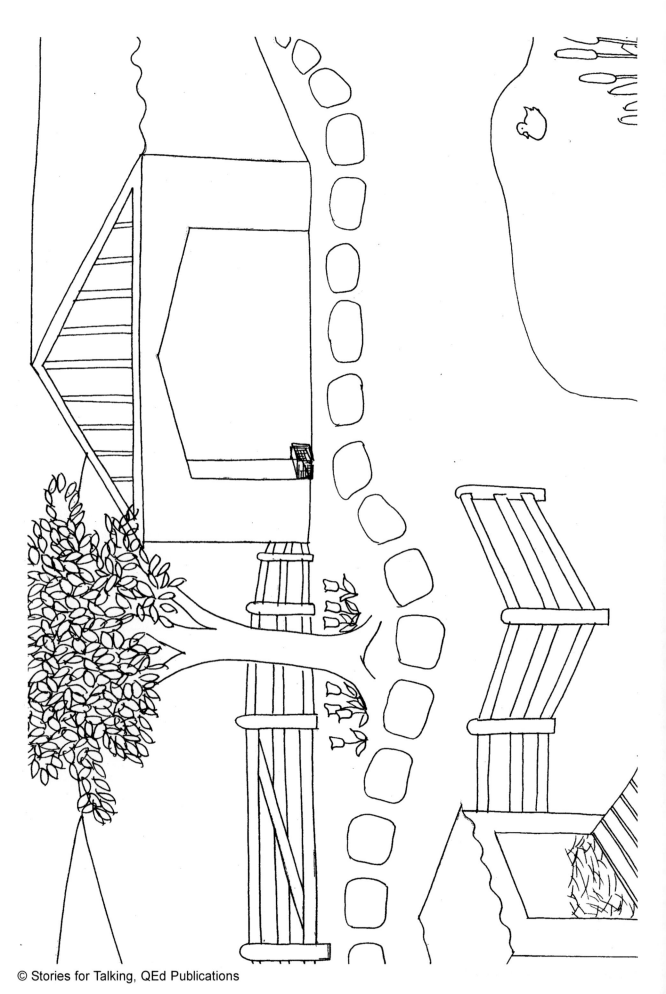

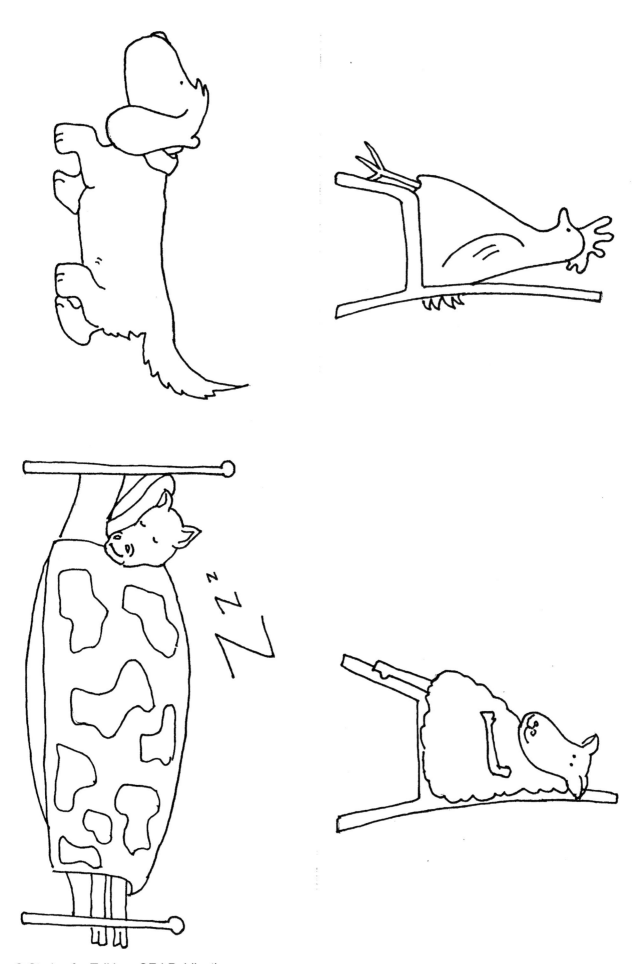

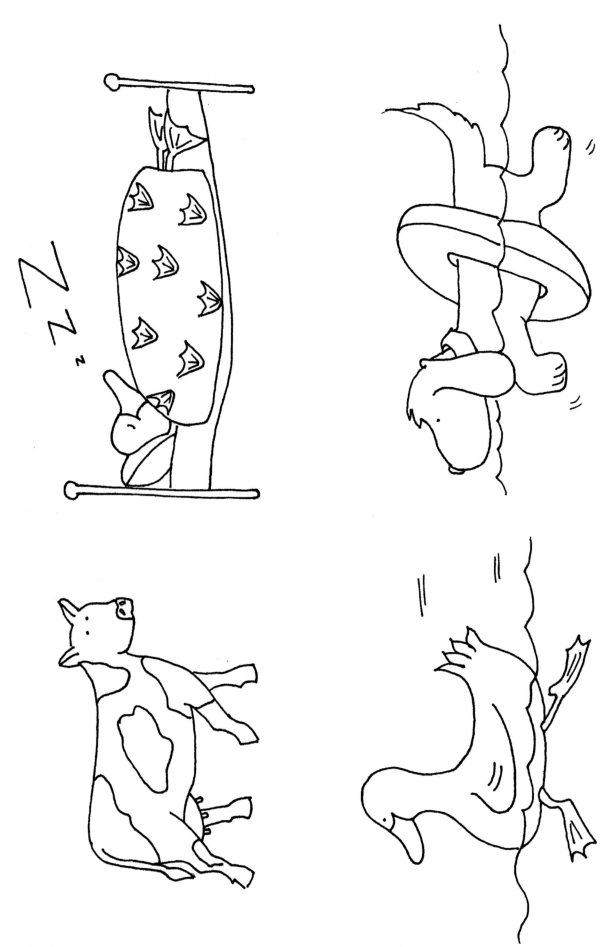

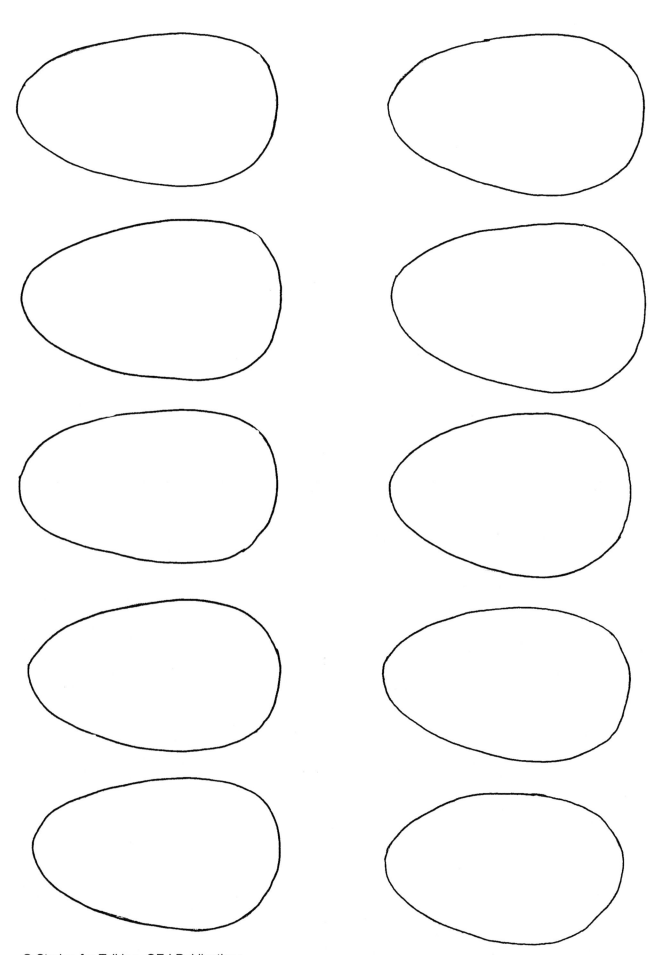

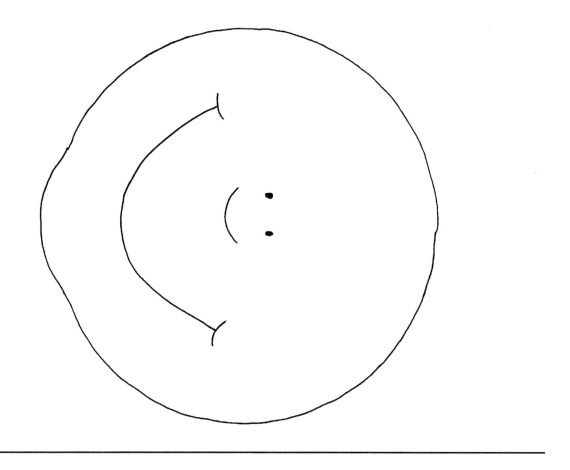

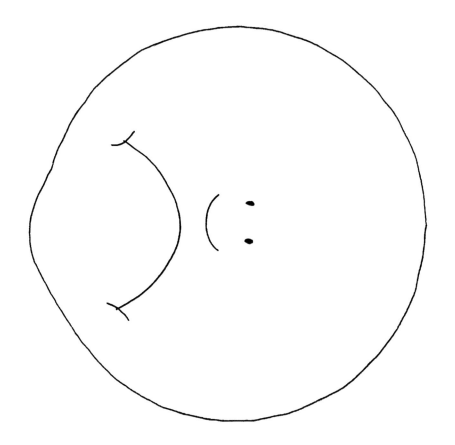

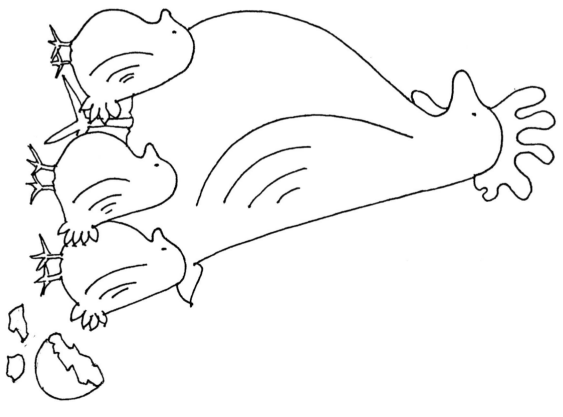

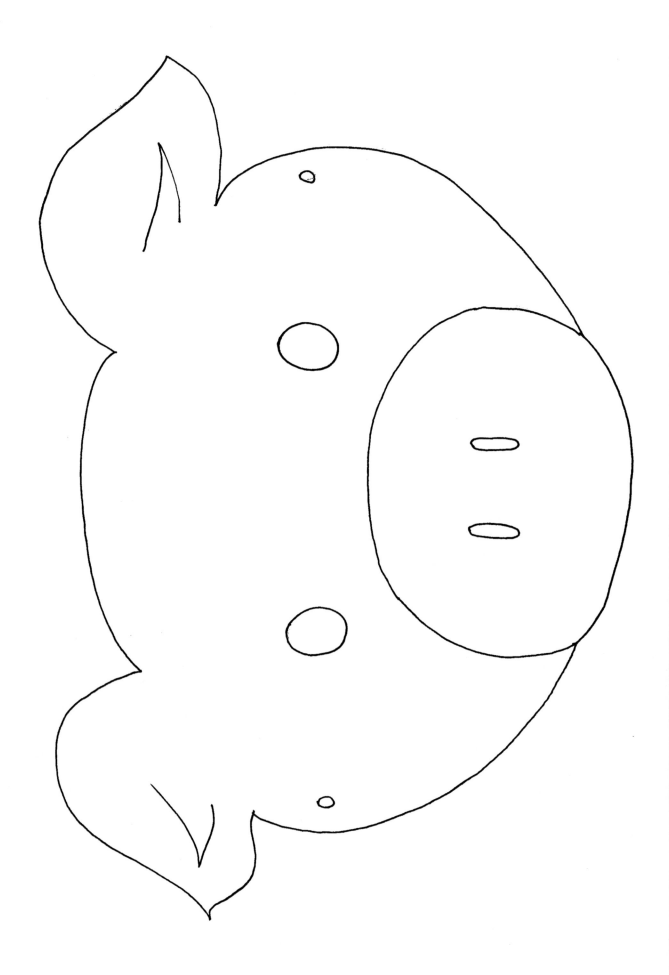

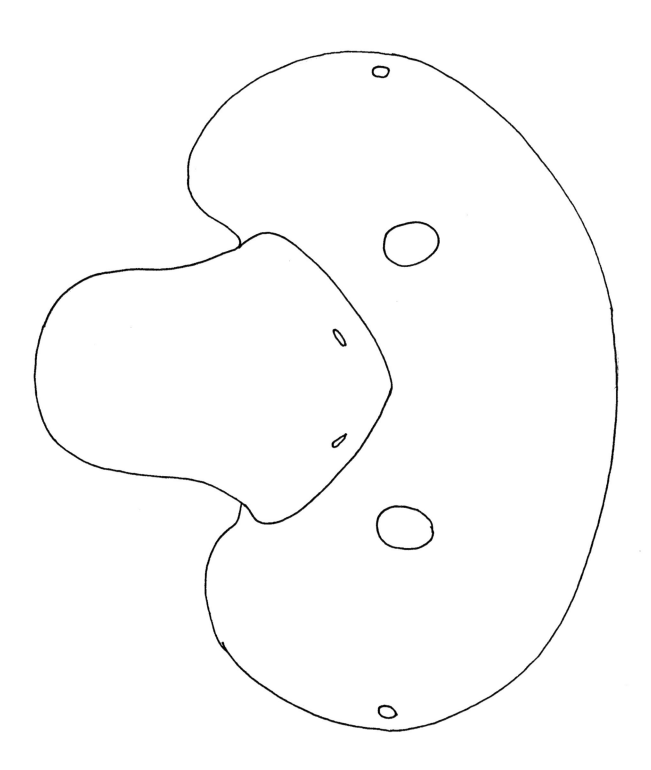

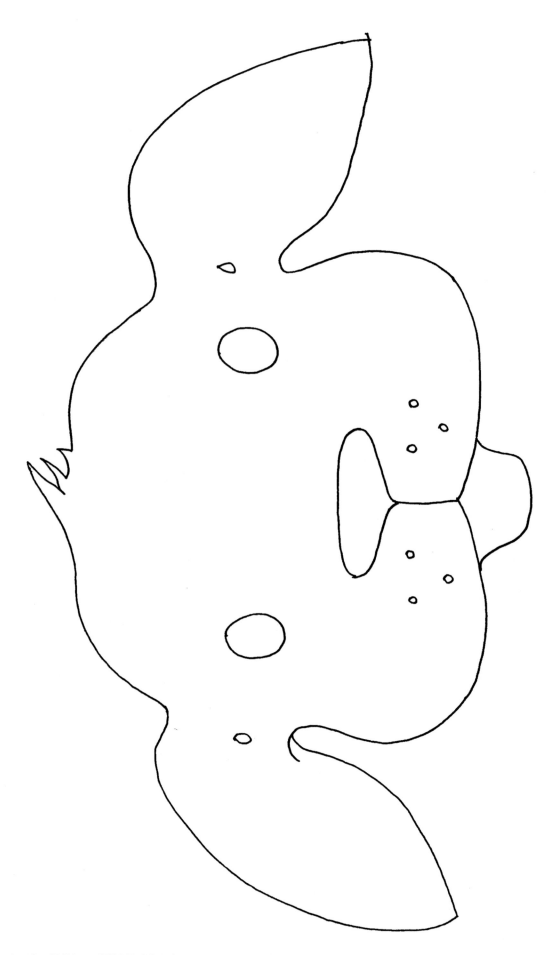

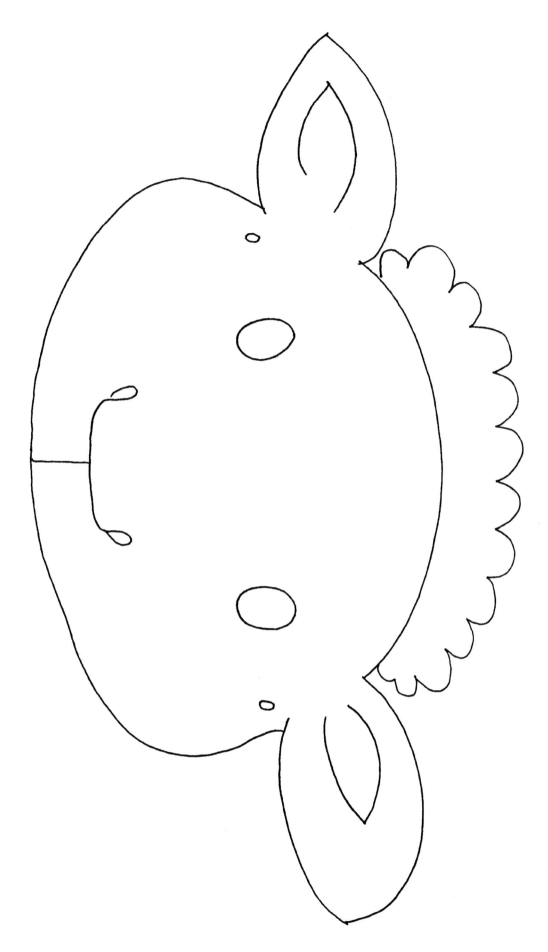

Goldilocks and the Three Bears

Section index

Goldilocks and the Three Bears

73

Section index continued

Goldilocks and the Three Bears

Level 1 – Introducing vocabulary

Topic category	Things in our homes
Nouns (object words) – basic level	**bowl** **chair** **fork** **table** **spoon** **bed** **knife** **cup** **porridge** **plate**
Notes	Whilst 'porridge' is not a household item, it has been included in the list of basic object vocabulary as it is so central to the story. The first five words appear in the book. 'Fork', 'knife', 'plate', 'table' and 'cup' do not feature in the book and have been added to complete the set of ten object words as they are other well known household items.
Verbs (action words)	**walking** **sitting** **running** **eating** **sleeping**
Concepts	**big** **little**
Notes	The three bears carry the description of 'father' who is 'big', 'mother' who is 'medium-sized' and 'baby' who is a 'tiny, little bear'. During the language activities which follow on from the story, it is important to focus on the pair of concepts 'big' and 'little'. Put less emphasis on 'tiny' as this may confuse a child who has not yet established the basic concept of 'little'. Also, omit the term 'medium-sized' in language activities as this concept is too difficult for children who have not yet grasped early concepts.
Parts of a whole vocabulary	There are no further, harder vocabulary items as there is no 'parts of a whole' vocabulary appropriate to this topic and these activities.

Story: Goldilocks and the Three Bears

Topic: Things in our homes

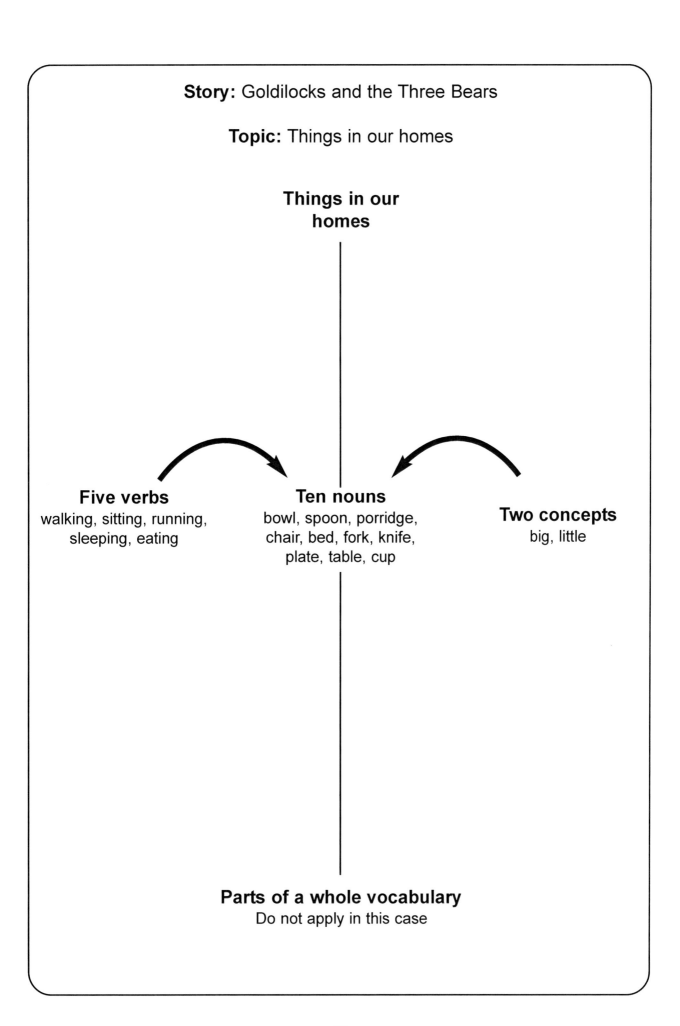

Things in our homes

Five verbs
walking, sitting, running, sleeping, eating

Ten nouns
bowl, spoon, porridge, chair, bed, fork, knife, plate, table, cup

Two concepts
big, little

Parts of a whole vocabulary
Do not apply in this case

Weekly plan for Level 1 – Introducing vocabulary

Goldilocks

Monday	
Focus	**Understanding object words**
What you need	Objects, both real and toy, to match the 10 chosen object words.
Activity 1	Read the story. As you read, encourage the children to have a turn at finding the object and matching it to the picture in the book. Make a point of saying the name of the household object a number of times – and if you know how, sign it too.
Activity 2	Lay out the objects on the floor and ask each child in turn to find one. For example: 'Laura, find me a spoon'; 'Jacob, find me a table'.
Notes	Remember, each day when you read the story you will be pointing out and emphasising all of the key vocabulary as it appears in the story and pictures. All of the vocabulary is therefore mentioned each day, but on certain days the activities and resources you use will particularly focus on one of the different word classes.
Tuesday	
Focus	**Naming object words**
What you need	Objects (as used on Monday). A 'feely bag' – an interesting bag, preferably with a drawstring top.
Activity 1	Pass the 'feely bag' around the group. Each child has a turn to reach inside the bag, pull out a household object and try to name it.
Activity 2	Read the story. Pause and leave a gap for children to name the household object as it appears in the story.
Wednesday	
Focus	**Understanding verbs (action words)**
What you need	A doll with blonde hair (to represent Goldilocks), a bed, chair, bowl and a spoon (to scale with the doll).
Activity 1	Read the story. As you come across each of the chosen five verbs in the story, act them out and get the group to copy you. You may need to add to the language of the book. For example when Goldilocks tastes the porridge, it is important to stress that she is 'eating'. When she 'tries out the beds' you need to use and stress the word 'sleeping' to clarify the meaning.
Activity 2	Place Goldilocks, the bed, chair, bowl and spoon in font of the children. Pass Goldilocks around the group. Say: 'Make Goldilocks eat', 'Make Goldilocks sleep/sit/run/ walk' and so on. Encourage each child to have a turn at making Goldilocks do the action you describe.

Weekly plan for Level 1 (continued)	*Goldilocks*
Thursday	
Focus	**Naming verbs (action words)**
What you need	Verb cards (photocopy page 88 twice). Bears for 'Hunt the Bear' game (photocopy page 91).
Activity 1	Read the story. Leave gaps and prompt the children to tell you what Goldilocks is doing on each page.
Activity 2	Use the verb cards that refer to Goldilocks performing an action: Goldilocks eating; Goldilocks sleeping; Goldilocks sitting; Goldilocks running; Goldilocks walking. Play 'Hunt the Bear' – put the verb cards face down, scattered across the floor. Hide a picture of a bear underneath some of the verb cards. Each child takes it in turns to turn a verb card over and say what Goldilocks is doing in the picture. If there is a bear hiding underneath, make Goldilocks 'run away'.
Friday	
Focus	**Understanding and naming concepts**
What you need	A big, a medium-sized and a little bear. Big, medium sized and little objects from the story (so as to match the bears).
Activity 1	Read the story, putting emphasis on 'big' and 'little' items and use sign and tone of voice to emphasise the concepts of 'big' and 'little'. Do not focus on 'middle-size' – just read it and pass on.
Activity 2	Set up Mummy bear and all her medium-sized objects to the side of you, away from the children's main area of attention, but where it is still easy to show them. Put the big and little bear in front of you, together with their big and little objects, all arranged at random. Explain that the Mummy bear has all her things (show them the middle-sized bear with all her middle-sized objects) but Daddy bear and Baby bear have got in a muddle – all their things have got mixed up and they need the children to help sort them out. Each child has a turn to choose an object – they must say whether it is 'big' or 'little' (encourage them to work out the other related item to give a comparison/idea of scale). If a child is struggling or gets it wrong, give them a choice (giving the correct answer as the second choice) with lots of over emphasising the correct word and gesture. For example, if it is a little spoon, say: 'Do you think it's big or <u>little</u>?' (Make sure to use a 'little' voice and gesture). If the object is a big chair, say: 'Do you think it's little or <u>big</u>?' (Using a 'big' voice and gesture when you ask the question).
Parent/carer activity	Hunt the Bear (as on Thursday).

Weekly plan for Level 2a – Building phrases and sentences – two words together

Monday	
Focus	**Modelling two word phrases**
What you need	Verb cards (photocopy pages 88-89).
Activity 1	Read the story. Model the two word phrases as you read. For example: 'bear walking'; 'Goldilocks sitting'; 'Goldilocks sleeping' and so on.
Activity 2	Go through the story again and match the verb cards to the pictures in the story. You can extend the activity by adding 'bear eating/sitting/sleeping'. Pretend that the bears did more than 'look' at the bowls, chairs and beds. For example, you could say that they ate some porridge, sat down, slept in the bed, and then said the 'Who's been . . . ?' line. This way you can involve the verb pictures of the bears to model a greater range of two word phrases.
Tuesday	
Focus	**Two key word comprehension**
What you need	A doll to represent Goldilocks, one bear, a chair, bed, and a bowl.
Activity 1	Read the story, modelling the two word phrases.
Activity 2	Comprehension activity at a two key word level. Use the toys and ask each child in turn to make 'Goldilocks sleep'; make 'bear sit'; make 'bear run'; make 'Goldilocks eat'. Use the different verb words 'walk', 'eat', 'sit', 'sleep', 'run' from the target vocabulary with the names 'bear' and 'Goldilocks' in your directions.
Wednesday	
Focus	**Two key word comprehension**
What you need	Verb cards (as on Monday). Small pictures of porridge (photocopy page 90).
Activity 1	Read the story, modelling the two word phrases.
Activity 2	Expressive language activity: 'Hunt the Porridge'. Place the verb cards face down, hiding porridge pictures under some of the pictures. The children take turns to choose a card, turn it over, say what's on it, for example: 'bear sleeping'. If they find some porridge, they keep it – the winner is the child with the most porridge at the end of the game.

Weekly plan for Level 2a (continued)	*Goldilocks*
Thursday	
Focus	**Expressive language activity**
What you need	Verb cards. A doll to represent Goldilocks, one bear, a chair, bed, and a bowl.
Activity 1	Read the story, modelling the two word phrases.
Activity 2	Choose a child who will be assigned the role of 'teacher' and ask them to choose a friend. First, 'Teacher' picks a verb card and then tells their friend what is on it, for example, 'Goldilocks sleeping'. The friend then acts this out with the toys. Both the 'teacher' and the friend, will need support. The 'teacher' may need help to construct the sentence and the friend may need prompting to listen and may also need you to repeat the direction again for them. Take it in turns so that each child has had a chance to be both a 'teacher' and a 'friend'.
Friday	
Focus	**Expressive language activity**
What you need	Verb cards. A doll to represent Goldilocks, one bear, a chair, bed, and a bowl.
Activity 1	Repeat the activity from Thursday. Hopefully, the children will require less prompting and support from you.
Parent/carer activity	Photocopy the verb pictures (see pages 88-89) and the pictures of porridge (page 90). Send home the 'Hunt the Porridge' game (as played on Wednesday).

Weekly plan for Level 2b – Building phrases and sentences – three words together	*Goldilocks*
Notes	These activities are for children who usually use short two or three word phrases and have a good vocabulary for basic objects. The following activities are to elicit three word sentences. Children at this level can also be encouraged to learn and join in the story with the 'Who's been . . . ?' line, which each bear repetitively says. Each day, when reading the story, put lots of emphasis (stress, tone of voice) into this line in the book. With repetition each day, the children may be able to 'help' you tell the story using this line. For example: 'Who's been eating my porridge?' etc.
Monday	
Focus	**Three key word comprehension**
What you need	A 'Goldilocks' doll, a bear, chair, bed, bowl and a spoon.
Activity 1	Read the story. Put lots of emphasis every time on the 'Who's been . . . ?' line.
Activity 2	Give an instruction, such as: 'Make Goldilocks sit in the bed' and encourage each child in turn to carry out the instruction. Other examples: 'Make Goldilocks jump on the chair'; 'Make Goldilocks sleep on the floor'; 'Make bear jump on the bed'; 'Make bear sleep on the bed'; 'Make bear sit on the floor'; 'Make Goldilocks sit in the bowl'. Make sure you give the children a variety of sentences and not just the usual ones, such as, 'sit on the chair', 'eat with the spoon', 'sleep on the bed'. These instructions do not require as much concentration and listening skills as the less typical ones like, 'sleep on the floor', or 'sit in the bowl'.
Tuesday	
Focus	**Expressive language activity**
What you need	Verb cards (photocopy pages 88-89). Pictures of porridge (photocopy page 90).
Activity 1	Read the story. Emphasise the 'Who's been . . . ?' line. Encourage the children to repeat it after you. Highlight the three word sentences shown in the book. For example: 'Look, Goldilocks is sleeping in the bed!'; 'Look, bear is eating the porridge!'
Activity 2	'Hunt the Porridge'. Turn the verb pictures face down, spread across the floor. Hide a porridge picture under some of the cards. Each child has a turn to get a card, describe the picture, for example: 'Bear sleeping in a bed'. If the child also gets a porridge picture he/she can keep it – the winner is the child with the most porridge at the end.

Wednesday	
Focus	**Listening and understanding language**
What you need	One 'Goldilocks' mask and one bear mask (photocopy pages 92-93). A child-sized bowl, chair and make a child-sized 'bed' on the floor with pillows and a blanket.
Activity 1	Read the story. Model the three word sentences as you read (as on Tuesday). Emphasise the 'Who's been . . ?' line, but this time leave a pause to prompt the children to finish off the question.
Activity 2	Listening activity. Use the masks and chair, bed and bowl. Give each child a turn to choose either a Goldilocks or a bear mask. When they are ready and listening, give the children an instruction, such as: 'Goldilocks, sleep in the chair'; 'Bear, eat on the bed'. As with the three key-word comprehension activity (from Monday), try to use a variety of typical and less typical actions, as this will encourage the children to listen more carefully.
Thursday	
Focus	**Expressive language**
What you need	Goldilocks mask and big bear mask (photocopy pages 92-93). Mummy bear mask and baby bear mask (photocopy pages 94-95). A child-sized bowl, chair and make a child-sized 'bed' on the floor with pillows and a blanket (as used on Wednesday).
Activity 1	Read the story, but first choose three of the most confidant children to be 'Daddy' 'Mummy' and 'Baby' bear wearing their masks. During the story, pause at the 'Who's been . . ?' line and prompt each bear to say their line. Keep modelling three word sentences throughout the story, as you're looking at the pictures. Now you need to begin to add 'big' and 'little' in too, for example: 'Look, here's Goldilocks sitting in the little chair'; 'Look, here's Goldilocks sleeping in the big bed'.
Activity 2	Use just the Goldilocks mask, one bear mask and the other props for this activity. Choose two children – one child will use a mask, the other child will be the 'teacher'. Once the child is wearing the mask, the 'teacher' will give him a direction, such as, 'bear, sit on the bed'. Both the 'teacher' and the friend will need support from you. The 'teacher' may need help to construct the sentence and the friend may need prompting to listen. You might also need to repeat the direction again for them. Take it in turns so that each child has a chance to be both a 'teacher' and a 'friend'.

Weekly plan for Level 2b (continued) *Goldilocks*

Friday	
Focus	**Expressive language**
What you need	Goldilocks mask and big bear mask (photocopy pages 92-93); mummy bear mask and baby bear mask (photocopy pages 94-95); one large child-sized 'bed' (as used on Thursday) and a smaller bed; big and little bowls; big and little chairs.
Activity 1	Read the story. This time, choose three different children to wear the masks and take part in the story (as done on Thursday).
Activity 2	Repeat the same activity as yesterday with two children, one being the 'teacher' and the other being the 'friend'. This time the aim is to encourage the children to give directions which include the words 'big' and 'little', for example: 'Bear, sit on the little chair'; 'Goldilocks, sleep on the big bed'; 'Goldilocks eat from the big bowl'. You may need to (a) model this longer sentence structure before you begin, and (b) help the child to decide what props they want to direct their friend to, before she or he begins to try and put the sentence together. For example: **Teacher:** 'Look! George has chosen to be Goldilocks. What shall Goldilocks do?' **Child:** 'Sit on the chair'. **Teacher:** 'Sit on the big chair or the little chair?' **Child:** 'Little chair'. **Teacher:** 'So you want Goldilocks to sit on the little chair. Can you tell Goldilocks what to do?'
Parent/carer activity	1) Hunt the Porridge game (as on Tuesday), making three word sentences using the verb cards (photocopy pages 88-90).

Weekly plan for Level 3 – Narrative	*Goldilocks*
Notes	The aim of this level is to give children an opportunity to experiment with creative story telling, develop combinations of two, three or more sentences, and develop an understanding and use of sequencing. Clearly, it is not suitable for children who have only recently begun to combine words in sentences.
Monday	
Focus	**Sequencing – matching pictures**
What you need	Sequencing pictures (photocopy pages 98-99).
Activity 1	Read the story.
Activity 2	Go back through the story and match the sequencing pictures to the corresponding part of the story. This will enable the children to lay out the sequencing cards in order.
Activity 3	Re-tell the story (in brief) from the sequencing strip of pictures. Use cue-cards and 'who?', 'where?', and 'what happened?' to prompt.
Tuesday	
Focus	**Sequencing – using memory**
What you need	Sequencing pictures (as on Monday).
Activity 1	Read the story.
Activity 2	Without using the book, see if the children can sequence the pictures in order.
Activity 3	Re-tell the story from the sequencing strip.
Wednesday	
Focus	**Retelling the story with toys**
What you need	Sequencing pictures; toy bears; Goldilocks doll; chairs, beds and bowls.
Activity 1	Read the story.
Activity 2	Sequence the pictures.
Activity 3	Use the toys to act out and re-tell the story. Give each child one of the bears, the Goldilocks doll or a piece of furniture. Encourage them to re-enact the story using the toys as props, taking turns to ask 'what happened next?' Use the sequencing pictures to prompt if a child has difficulty.

Thursday	
Focus	**Creating a new story**
What you need	Toy bears, 'Goldilocks' doll, chairs, beds and bowls of different sizes.
Activity 1	Read the story.
Activity 2	Model how to create a different story, making sure you tell the children what you're doing: 'I'm going to tell a different story about Goldilocks and the Three Bears'. For example: 'Goldilocks goes to the bears' house and they are in. They invite her to join them for breakfast. 'Come and have some of my porridge', said Daddy Bear. 'Come and sit in my chair', said Mummy Bear. At the end of the day Goldilocks was very tired and had a sleep in Baby Bear's bed.'
Friday	
Focus	**Creating a new story**
What you need	Goldilocks, bears and other cuddly toys. Various other household objects such as forks, knives, cups, as well as bowls, beds and chairs.
Activity 1	**Don't** read the story! You and the children will create your own story this time.
Activity 2	Start the story off. Each child has a turn to take a toy and try to tell a small part of the story. Make sure that you connect each part of the story and give it an ending. Do not worry if the children go off at a tangent, become repetitive, don't make logical suggestions or make up an exciting story. Initially, it is just about the children having an opportunity to be creative, expressing basic ideas and learning to take turns at being the storyteller.
Parent/carer activity	Photocopy the sequencing strip for Goldilocks on pages 98-99 and send this home for them to practise sequencing and telling the story.

Goldilocks – generalising language and skills within the EYFS	
Notes	Generalising the language and skills taught throughout other activities in the EYFS gives essential opportunities for **repetition** and **functional** use of language to improve social skills and confidence. Here are some examples of activities to build on the language of Goldilocks and the Three Bears.
Snack time Personal, Social and Emotional Development – Self-care	Have cereal or porridge requiring bowls and spoons. Get groups of children to lay the table with cups, bowls and spoons.
Sand tray Problem Solving, Reasoning and Numeracy – Shape, Space and Measures	Have 'porridge oats' with big and little spoons, big and little pans, big and little cups, forks, plates and so on.
Cooking corner Creative Development – Exploring Media and Materials	Stick a plate/bowl on some paper, together with a spoon, knife and fork like a table setting. You could also stick oats, lentils, seeds or dried pasta on the plate and make a collage. Provide pictures or outline drawings of a spoon, knife, fork, plate and cup and encourage the children to stick them on a card in the appropriate places. Decorate them, laminate and allow children to take them home as a place mat.
Painting Creative Development – Being Creative	Have big and little pieces of paper available to choose and paint on. Paint a plate, letting the child choose between a big or little plate.
Home corner Problem Solving, Reasoning and Numeracy – Calculating	Provide a bag of big and little objects, preferably using objects in the targeted vocabulary (bowl, spoon, cup, plate and so on) and encourage the children to sort them.
Water tray Problem Solving, Reasoning and Numeracy – Shape, Space and Measures	Provide big and little kitchen containers and utensils for pouring and ladling.
Construction Knowledge and Understanding of the World – Designing and Making	Use varying types and sizes of construction materials to make beds and chairs for the three bears, such as Lego for little bear, large plastic bricks for Mummy bear and very large wooden bricks for Daddy bear. Facilitate groups of children to plan, build and problem solve together.
Home corner Problem Solving, Reasoning and Numeracy – Calculating	Provide masks and dressing up clothes for Goldilocks and the three bears. Provide different sized beds, chairs, bowls and spoons. Put placemats with different sizes of spoons, knifes and folks on the table, for matching.
Small world play	Put small bears and a blonde-haired doll in a dolls house instead of the usual dolls.
Outdoor play Communication, Language and Literacy – Language for Communication	Play Simon Says using the five verbs targeted as your commands (walk, eat, sit sleep, run). After modelling it yourself, encourage the children to take turns to be 'Simon' and give directions. Alternatively, play the same game but call it 'Big Bear Says' and give the child a bear mask to wear when it is his/her turn to give a direction.

Goldilocks – generalising language and skills within the EYFS	
Interactive displays	**1) Sorting activity** Cut out, laminate and Velcro the three bears from the pictures (photocopy page 97). Cut out and laminate different sized household objects (bowl, chair, fork, table, spoon, bed, knife, cup, plate) from catalogues, magazines and so on. Allow the children to sort out objects for each of the three bears. **2) House activity** Use a large basic outline of a house and stick pictures of beds, chairs, tables etc on it (cut up catalogues for these). Laminate and put velcro on the key items of furniture. Cut out and laminate pictures of the three bears and Goldilocks (photocopy page 96) and encourage the children to put them in different places around the house and describe what each is doing.
Sticky pictures	There are some available commercially of houses with furniture to stick on.

Photocopiable Resources
for
Goldilocks and the Three Bears

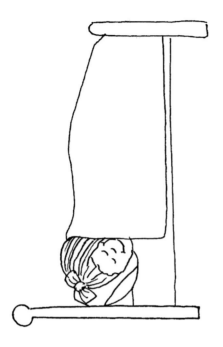

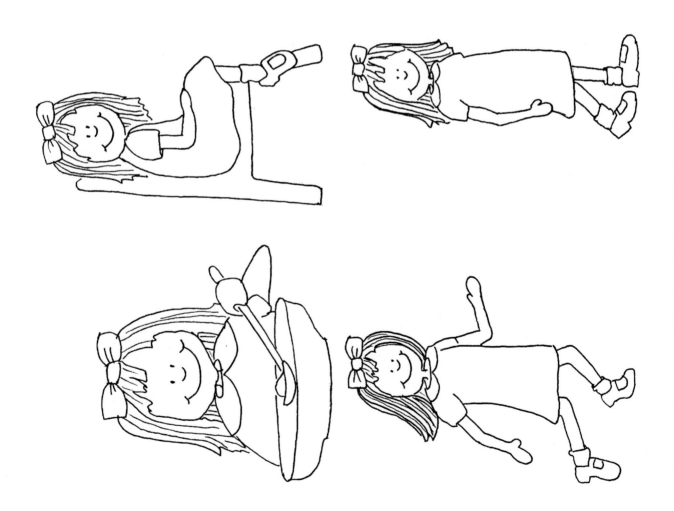

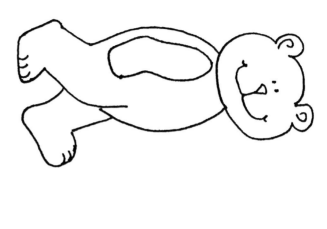

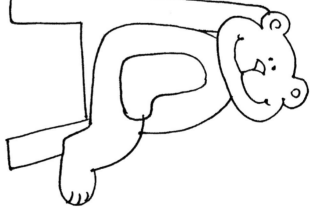

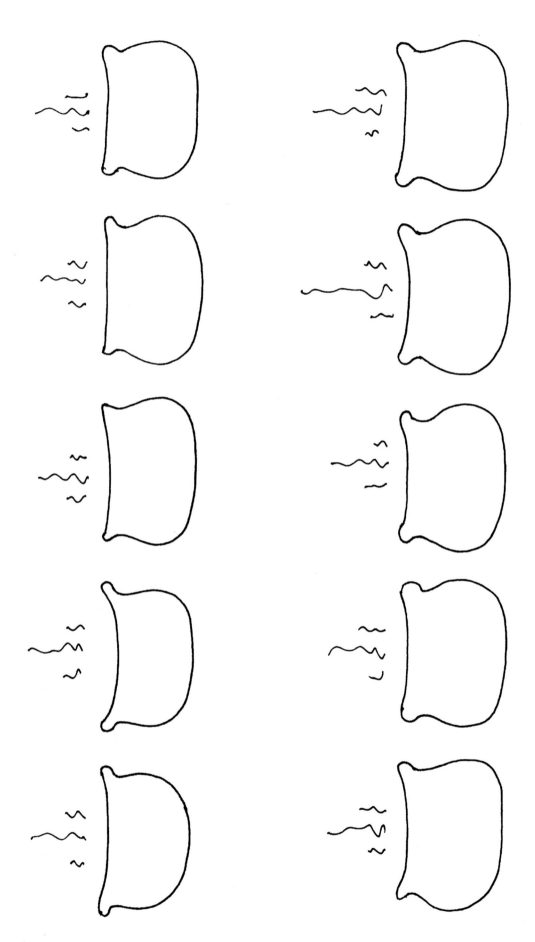

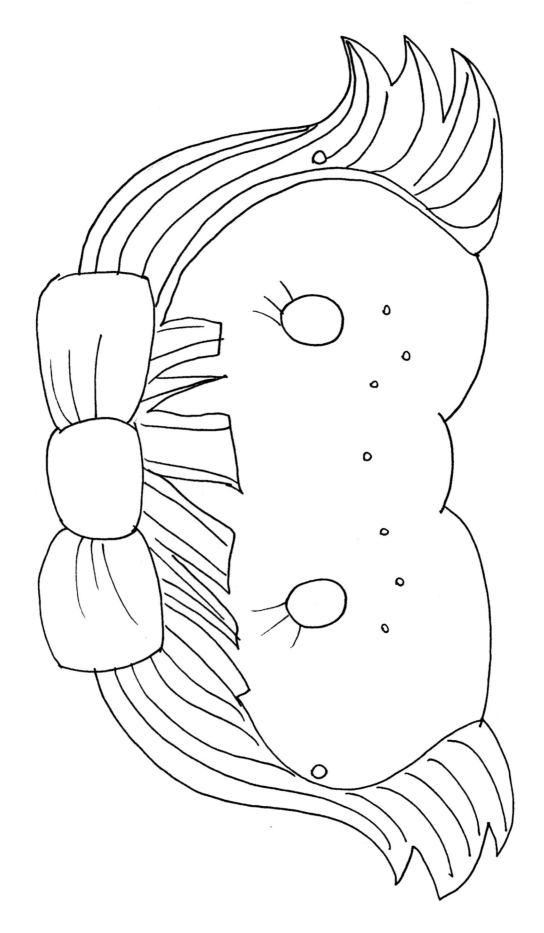

Washing Line

by Jez Alborough

Section index

Washing Line

Section index continued

Washing Line

Level 1 – Introducing vocabulary

Topic category	Clothes
Nouns (object words) – basic level	**socks** **dress** **pants** **jumper** **scarf** **trousers** **coat** **T-shirt** **hat** **shorts**
Notes	Whilst animals feature heavily in the story, their names are not in the target vocabulary list as these activities are designed to focus on teaching the category of 'clothes'. The first five words appear in the book. 'trousers', 'coat', 'T-shirt', 'hat' and 'shorts' do not feature in the book and have been added to complete the set of ten object words.
Verbs (action words)	**wearing** **washing** **drying** **hanging** **splashing**
Concepts	**wet** **dry**
Notes	These concepts are central to the story and can be easily taught and reinforced in activities involving clothes.
Parts of a whole vocabulary	**hood** **collar** **button** **sleeve** **pocket** **belt** **cuff** **zip** **laces** **Velcro strip** Remember this is only taught to children who have a good grasp of the basic vocabulary and are able to both understand and label (say) the basic words listed earlier.

Story: Washing Line

Topic: Clothes

Clothes

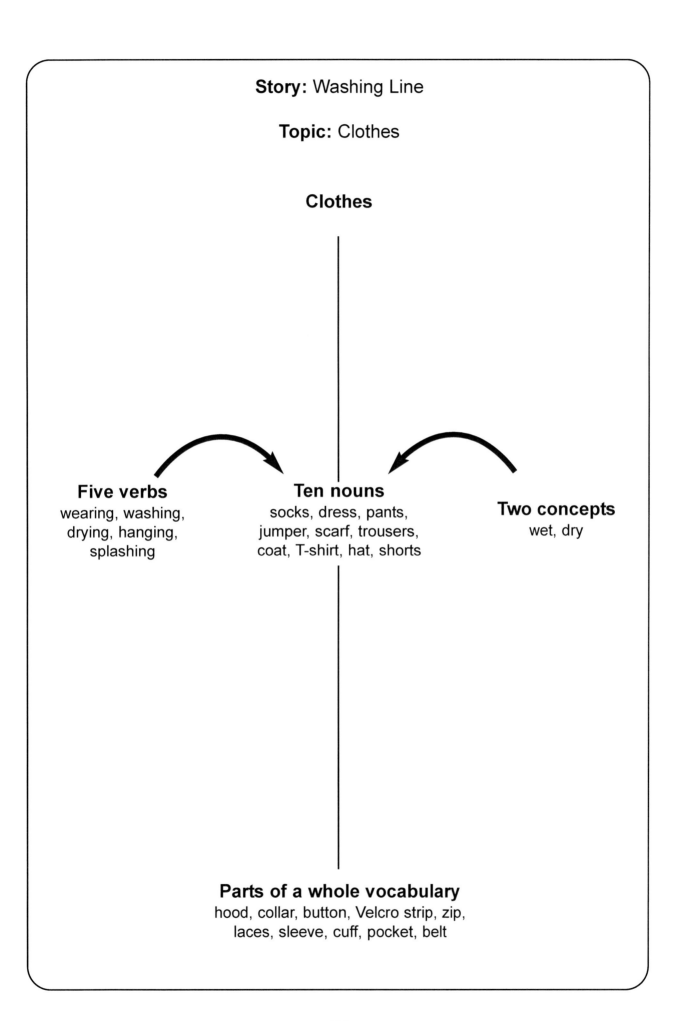

Five verbs
wearing, washing,
drying, hanging,
splashing

Ten nouns
socks, dress, pants,
jumper, scarf, trousers,
coat, T-shirt, hat, shorts

Two concepts
wet, dry

Parts of a whole vocabulary
hood, collar, button, Velcro strip, zip,
laces, sleeve, cuff, pocket, belt

Weekly plan for Level 1 – Introducing vocabulary

Washing Line

Monday	
Focus	**Understanding object words**
What you need	Clothes (preferably child-sized ones) to represent the 10 chosen clothes words (socks, dress, pants, jumper, scarf, trousers, coat, T-shirt, hat, shorts). A big cardboard box, cut and decorated to look like a washing machine or a toy washing machine from the home corner area of your nursery.
Activity 1	Read the story. As you read, encourage the children to have a turn at finding the object and matching it to the picture in the book. Make a point of saying the name of the item of clothing a number of times – and point to the same items the children are wearing. Introduce the other five items of clothing that do not appear in the book, repeating the word lots of times, and pointing out these items if any of the children are wearing them.
Activity 2	Lay out all of the clothes on the floor near to the washing machine. Encourage each child to have a turn at finding an item of clothing at your request and then putting it in the washer. For example: 'Tracy, find the socks. Good, can you put them in the washer, please?'
Notes	Remember, each day when you read the story you will be pointing out and emphasising all of the key vocabulary as it appears in the story and pictures. All of the vocabulary is therefore mentioned each day, but on certain days the activities and resources you use will particularly focus on one of the different word classes.
Tuesday	
Focus	**Naming object words**
What you need	A selection of real clothes (as used on Monday); a washing line across the room at child height; some pegs; a toy washing machine or converted cardboard box (as used on Monday).
Activity 1	Read the story, pausing at the name of the clothes items to give the children a chance to name the clothes.
Activity 2	Have the clothes already in the 'washing machine': Tell the children that the clothes have just finished washing and need hanging on the line to dry. Each child takes a turn to pull an item of clothing from the washer, name it, and peg it on the washing line. If the child is struggling to name the item, offer them a choice. For example, Liam pulls a scarf from the washer but is unable to tell you what it is. You say: 'is it some pants or a <u>scarf</u>?' (putting emphasis on the word scarf).

Weekly plan for Level 1 (continued)	*Washing Line*
Wednesday	
Focus	**Understanding verbs (action words)**
What you need	A washing basket; washing line and pegs; a toy/cardboard washing machine (as used on Monday and Tuesday); some real children's sized clothes (as used on Monday and Tuesday).
Activity 1	Read the story. As you read it, highlight and talk about what you can see the animals doing in each picture, for example, wearing, hanging, splashing and so on.
Activity 2	Put the clothes in the washing basket. Give each child a turn at choosing an item of clothing. He/she may name it or you can remind them of the name, or give a choice. Give the child a little instruction to understand and follow, for example: 'Bella, can you dry the sock?'; 'Tyler, can you wash the scarf?'; 'Joshua, can you wear the jumper?' If the instruction is 'wash', encourage the child to put the item of clothing in the washing machine. If the instruction is 'wear' they can choose either to put on the item (if simple, like a scarf) or they can hold the item up against their body. If dry, encourage the children to peg the clothes items on the line.
Thursday	
Focus	**Naming verbs (action words)**
What you need	Verb cards (photocopy pages 118-119); washing line and pegs.
Activity 1	Read the story. Once again comment on and emphasise the action words in the story and portrayed in the pictures.
Activity 2	Peg the verb cards on the washing line with the picture facing away from the children. Each child has a turn to unpeg a picture and describe what the animal is doing, for example: 'Wearing scarf'; 'Washing socks'; 'Drying trousers'. It is highly likely that the child will look at the picture and name the clothing item not the action word. For example they might say 'socks' but not 'washing'. When this happens you can help by agreeing and then prompt them to say the action words: 'Yes, he's got socks. What's he doing to the socks?'. If necessary, offer a choice: 'Is he <u>wearing</u> the socks or <u>washing</u> the socks?'. 'Wearing' is the harder verb and also the least obvious in a picture, so this is likely to need prompting.

Friday	
Focus	**Understanding and naming concepts**
What you need	Children's clothes (some wet, some dry); a washing line; two washing up bowls/washing baskets.
Activity 1	Read the story. Emphasise the idea of the clothes being dry and ready to wear, then getting wet at the end.
Activity 2	The selection of wet and dry clothes should be hung on the washing line. Give each child a turn to choose and unpeg an item of clothing, feel it, and decide if it is 'wet' or 'dry'. Ask the children to sort the clothes into bowls of wet or dry clothes.
Parent/carer activity	Photocopy the picture of the washing line and clothes (pages 129-131). Ask the parent/carer to cut out the clothes, allowing the child to name them as they cut, and then stick them on the washing line.

Weekly plan for Level 2a – Building phrases and sentences – two words together	*Washing Line*
Monday	
Focus	**Two key word comprehension**
What you need	A selection of boys and girls clothes (such as jumpers, socks, trousers, hats). If possible, try to find clothes that are very obviously for boys and girls.
Activity 1	Read the story, emphasising the names of the clothes.
Activity 2	Lay out the clothes on the floor – ensure there is a boy's and girl's item for each piece of clothing. Each child has a turn to listen to an instruction and find the appropriate item: 'Find the boy's hat'; 'Find the girl's trousers'; 'Find the girl's scarf'.
Tuesday	
Focus	**Two key word comprehension**
What you need	Animals and clothes (photocopy pages 120-128) to cut out and colour in, and laminate if possible; Blu-Tac or Velcro.
Activity 1	Read the story, emphasising both the clothes words and animal words as you read.
Activity 2	Put the animal pictures on a wall/white board and lay the clothes pictures out on the floor. Give each child a turn at listening and carrying out your instructions. For example: 'John, give the <u>giraffe</u> a <u>scarf</u>'; 'Sasha, give the <u>mouse</u> a <u>hat</u>'. Note that certain clothes items should fit certain animals. This ensures that the child is not relying purely on his/her memory of what each animal wears in the book. Listed below are a choice of two items for each animal so that the child has to listen and understand both pieces of information in the instruction (choose the correct <u>animal</u> and the correct <u>clothes item</u>). **Elephant** – pants, T-shirt **Flamingo** – socks, coat **Monkey** – jumper, trousers **Mouse** – dress, hat **Giraffe** – scarf, shorts

Wednesday	
Focus	**Expressive language activity – saying two word phrases**
What you need	Laminated pictures of animals and clothes (as used on Monday); Blu-tac/Velcro.
Activity 1	Read the story.
Activity 2	As you read, give each child the opportunity to find the appropriate clothes for the animal as it appears in the book. The child can then stick the clothes on the animal and say which item of clothing is on the animal, for example: 'Scarf on giraffe'; 'Pants on elephant'; 'Dress on mouse'.
Thursday	
Focus	**Expressive language activity – giving two word instructions**
What you need	Real children's clothing; a washing line and pegs; washing machine (either a toy one, or made from a cardboard box).
Activity 1	Read the story.
Activity 2	Lay out the clothes across the floor. Each child has a turn to be the 'teacher' and chooses a friend to give a 'message' to. The 'teacher' must instruct their friend to put an item of clothing into the washer or on the line. For example, Amy chooses Lily. You help Amy to give the message to Lily: 'Lily, put the hat in the washer'.
Friday	
Focus	**Expressive language activity – giving two word instructions**
What you need	The animals and clothes laminated pictures (photocopied from pages 120-128, as used on Tuesday and Wednesday).
Activity 1	Read the story.
Activity 2	As on Thursday, give each child an opportunity to be the 'teacher' and choose a friend to give a message to. Today they must make up an instruction telling their friend which clothes to put on which animal. For example: 'Dylan, put the dress on the monkey'. The children may be less aware of which clothes fit which animals, resulting in some funny pictures, such as a tiny dress on a big monkey. Make a joke of this and talk about it. For example: 'Oh no! It's too big/little!'
Parent/carer activity	Photocopy the washing line and clothes on pages 129-131. The parent/carer can help the child cut out and stick the clothes on the line, and as they do this they should encourage the child to name them. For example: 'Daddy's socks'; 'girl's trousers', 'Mummy's T-shirt' and so on.

Weekly plan for Level 2b – Building phrases and sentences – three words together	*Washing Line*
Notes	These activities are for children who usually use two or three word phrases and have a good vocabulary for basic objects. The following activities are to elicit three word sentences.
Monday	
Focus	**Three key word comprehension**
What you need	A range of child sized clothes; a cardboard box cut and painted to look like a washing machine or a toy washing machine from the home corner.
Activity 1	Read the story. Put lots of emphasis on the names of the clothes items.
Activity 2	Lay the clothes out on the floor. Give each child a turn to listen to your instruction asking them to put three things into the washing machine. For example: 'Iqbal, put the <u>jumper</u>, the <u>sock</u> and the <u>pants</u> in the washing machine'; 'Emma, put the <u>coat</u>, the <u>scarf</u> and the <u>dress</u> in the washing machine'.
Tuesday	
Focus	**Three key word comprehension**
What you need	Pictures of animals and clothes, coloured and laminated, if possible (photocopy page 120-128); a washing line and pegs; a washing machine (either toy or made from cardboard, as used previously).
Activity 1	Read the story.
Activity 2	Lay out (or stick on the wall) the animal pictures all together and the clothes pictures all together. Give each child an opportunity to listen and follow your instructions; give the child an instruction to make an animal wear, wash or dry an item of clothing. For example: 'Elliot, make the <u>monkey</u> <u>wear</u> the <u>jumper</u>' (he should then stick the picture of the jumper onto the monkey); 'Molly, make the <u>mouse</u> <u>wash</u> the <u>trousers</u>' (she should then make the mouse put the trousers in the washing machine); 'Derris, make the <u>giraffe</u> <u>dry</u> the <u>socks</u>' (he should then make the giraffe get the socks and peg them on the washing line). It would be a good idea to model each of these types of sentences and actions before giving the children the instructions.

Wednesday	
Focus	**Expressive language – building three word sentences**
What you need	A ball.
Activity 1	Read the story.
Activity 2	Everyone (including you) sit on the floor in a circle. Give each child a turn to roll the ball to a friend, but first they must say the sentence: 'I'm wearing . . .' You should start the game off: 'I've got the ball. I'm going to say 'I'm wearing socks' (point to your socks). You roll the ball to Mia and ask 'Mia, what are you wearing?' Mia replies: 'Jumper'. 'Yes, so Mia can say, 'I'm wearing a jumper.'
Thursday	
Focus	**Expressive language – building three word sentences**
What you need	A bean bag or cuddly toy.
Activity 1	Read the story.
Activity 2	As on Wednesday, sit in a circle with the children. The game is the same (to throw the bean bag/toy to a friend), but this time the child has to comment on what their friend is wearing before throwing the bean bag to them. For example: 'John, its your turn – who will you choose?' 'Mia' 'And what's Mia wearing?' 'Socks' 'Yes, so you say 'Mia's wearing socks". Encourage the children to build their sentences independently, relying less on your prompts over the course of the game: 'Ann's wearing jumper'; 'Callum's wearing shoes'; 'William's wearing pants'.

Friday	
Focus	**Expressive language – building three word sentences**
What you need	Coloured and laminated pictures of animals and clothes (as used on Tuesday); Blu-Tac.
Activity 1	Read the story.
Activity 2	Explain that you cannot remember which animal wears what clothes. Put the clothes on the animals, but put them on incorrectly so that they don't fit (such as a tiny dress on elephant). Try to make a joke of what you are doing: 'Oh no! Is that right? think I've got it wrong. What should I do?' The aim is to get the children to tell you using a three word sentence, such as: 'Dress on mouse'; 'Jumper on monkey'; 'Scarf on giraffe'. It is likely that the children will all laugh and shout out what to do, so after this, ask one child to come out and tell you what to do to put it right. Make sure each child gets a turn.
Parent/carer activity	Ask the children to look at photos at home, or even just look around at their family members, and describe what each is wearing. For example: 'Mummy wearing trousers'; 'Nana wearing a dress'; 'Baby wearing a hat'.

Weekly plan for Level 3 – Narrative	*Washing Line*
Notes	The aim of this level is to give children an opportunity to experiment with creative story telling, develop combinations of two, three or more sentences, and develop an understanding and use of sequencing. This level is not suitable for children who have only recently begun to combine words in sentences.
Monday	
Focus	**Sequencing – matching pictures**
What you need	Sequencing pictures (photocopy page 132).
Activity 1	Read the story.
Activity 2	Go back through the story and match the sequencing pictures to the corresponding part of the story. This will enable the children to lay out the sequencing cards in order.
Activity 3	Re-tell the story (in brief) from the sequencing strip of pictures.
Tuesday	
Focus	**Sequencing – using memory**
What you need	Sequencing pictures washing line and pegs (as on Monday).
Activity 1	Read the story.
Activity 2	Show the children the sequencing pictures and see if they can recall the story, sequencing the pictures in the right order. Hang each picture on the washing line as you go along, recalling the story together.
Wednesday	
Focus	**Retelling the story**
What you need	A large board (Velcro/felt or white board); pictures of animals and clothes (photocopy pages 120-128), cut these out, colour them in and laminate, if possible. Attach either Velcro or Blu-Tac to make them stick on the interactive board.
Activity 1	Read the story.
Activity 2	Give each child a picture of an animal and re-enact the story together using the clothes and animals. Encourage all of the children to join in with the 'Whose is this hanging on the washing line?' and encourage each child to watch, listen and say 'It's mine', before sticking his/her animal on the board and making them wear their clothes item. Finish the story off at the end, where the elephant gets them all wet again.

Weekly plan for Level 3 (continued)	*Washing Line*
Thursday	
Focus	**Creating a new story**
What you need	Animals and clothes pictures and interactive board (as used on Wednesday).
Activity 1	**Don't** read the story! Instead, use the pictures on the board to create a different story involving the same animal characters and clothes. For example, talk through all the animals getting dressed on a morning and which clothes item each animal chooses. Explain that the animals then go out for a walk together (you could get each child to 'walk' a certain animal round the room), and then come to a muddy field and all fall down and get stuck in the mud. In the end they all have to go home and put their clothes in the wash again.
Friday	
Focus	**Creating a new story**
What you need	Materials as described in 'Interactive Display III' (see page 115); different pictures of clothes (such as those cut out from catalogues) laminated, if possible.
Activity 1	**Don't** read the story! You and the children will create your own story this time.
Activity 2	Encourage the children to make up their own story. Help them by starting the story: Tell the children that the story begins with them getting up in the morning and getting dressed. Each child can choose which items of clothing to match to her or his 'head' on the board. Encourage the children to talk about where they might go once they are dressed. They may choose somewhere as a group, or individuals may have different ideas – either way is fine. Then ask the children to think about what they each did, such as what happened at the place they chose to go to. Develop the story as little or as much as the children are able to, using prompts and questions. Be careful not to let the more able children dominate the activity, leaving no time for any less confident children to voice their ideas.
Parent/carer activity	Photocopy the sequencing pictures (page 132) used at the beginning of the week. Encourage the children to sequence the pictures and retell the story to their parents/people at home.

Washing Line – generalising language and skills within the EYFS

Notes	Generalising the language and skills taught throughout other activities in the EYFS gives essential opportunities for **repetition** and **functional** use of language to improve social skills and confidence. Here are some examples of activities to build on the language used in *Washing Line*. Under each activity heading are just some possible Focuses of Development within the Early Years Foundation Stage.
Water Personal, Social and Emotional Development – Self-care	Put a variety of clothes in the water with soap/soap flakes/bubbles/empty bottles of washing detergent. In the summer, this activity can be set up outdoors – you could also create a washing line to peg out the clothes.
Sand tray Creative Development – Exploring Media and Materials	Have two sand trays available, one 'wet' and one 'dry' to illustrate these concepts.
Designing and making Creative Development – Being Creative	Make clothes peg 'dolls'; create different figures with different clothes, and have lots of different types of fabric with which to 'design and create'.
Jigsaws Problem Solving, Reasoning and Numeracy – Shape, Space and Measures	Dressing jigsaws; sequencing jigsaws with clothes.
Home corner and role play Communication, Language and Literacy – Language for Thinking	Provide a toy washer, washing line, pegs and lots of clothes. Provide lots of dressing up clothes for children and dolls, especially a range of 'normal' clothes rather than just fancy dress/hats and so on.
Drawing and painting Knowledge and Understanding of the World – Exploration and Investigation	'This is me' – focus on the clothing that the child is wearing with lots of talk about their clothes. Talk about their paintings being 'wet' and 'dry'.
Snack time Physical Development – Using Equipment and Materials	The 'helper' has to wear a certain, special item of clothing e.g., jumper, hat, scarf, apron before serving snack or doing their special job.
Listening Personal, Social and Emotional Development – Self-care	Musical game where a child has a turn at putting on clothes such as a hat, gloves or scarf before eating chocolate/apple pieces etc. When the music stops, they have to stop eating and let somebody else have a turn.
Sequencing Communication, Language and Literacy – Language for Thinking	Make up repetitive patterns of different coloured clothes and stick them on a washing line, for example: red sock, blue sock, red sock, blue sock.
Books Personal, Social and Emotional Development – Self-care	Books with pictures of dressing sequence; other stories about clothes, washing, dressing up, for example *How do I put it on?* by Shingeo Wanabe. *Hippo has a Hat* by Julia Donaldson and Nick Sharratt. Story sacks. *The Washing Game* by Orchard Toys.

Washing Line – generalising language and skills within the EYFS	
Interactive displays	**1) Display I** Use a large board (felt/white board) with a washing line, animals and corresponding clothes (photocopy pages 120-128, colour in and attach Velcro/Blu-Tac). Children can take the clothes on and off the line and try them on the different animals. **2) Display II** Have a board covered with photos of the children, some taken at nursery and some brought from home, where they might be wearing special or favourite clothes or pyjamas. Discuss the different clothes the children are wearing and different clothes for different occasions. Use as a prompt to discuss what children are wearing on the day. **3) Display III** Take photos of the children. Cut out the heads, laminate, and stick on a large interactive display board along with lots of different pictures of clothes (cut and laminate pictures from catalogues). The children can play 'dressing up', and experiment with lots of different outfits to put with their face (like the 'misfits' game).

Photocopiable Resources
for
Washing Line

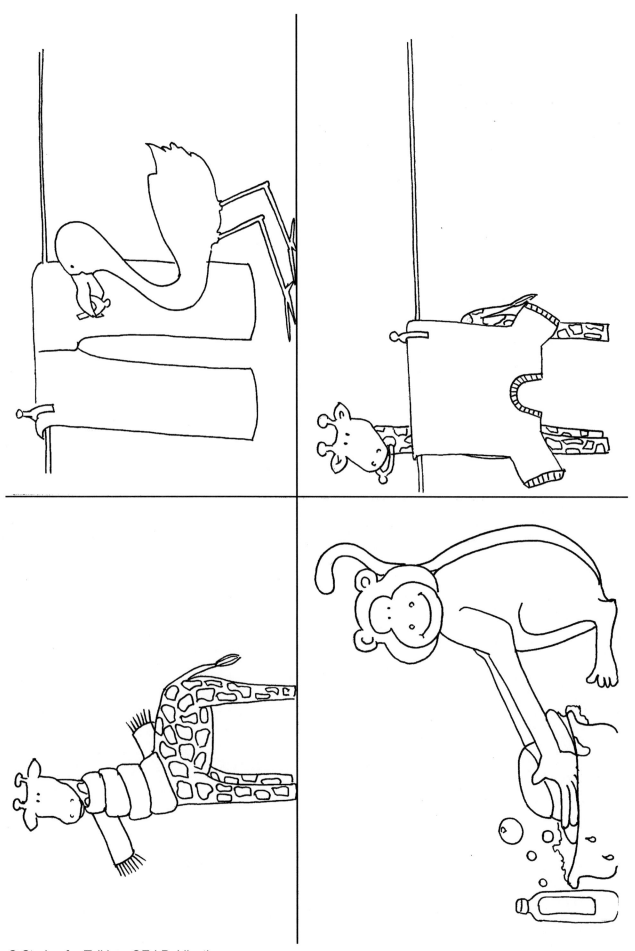

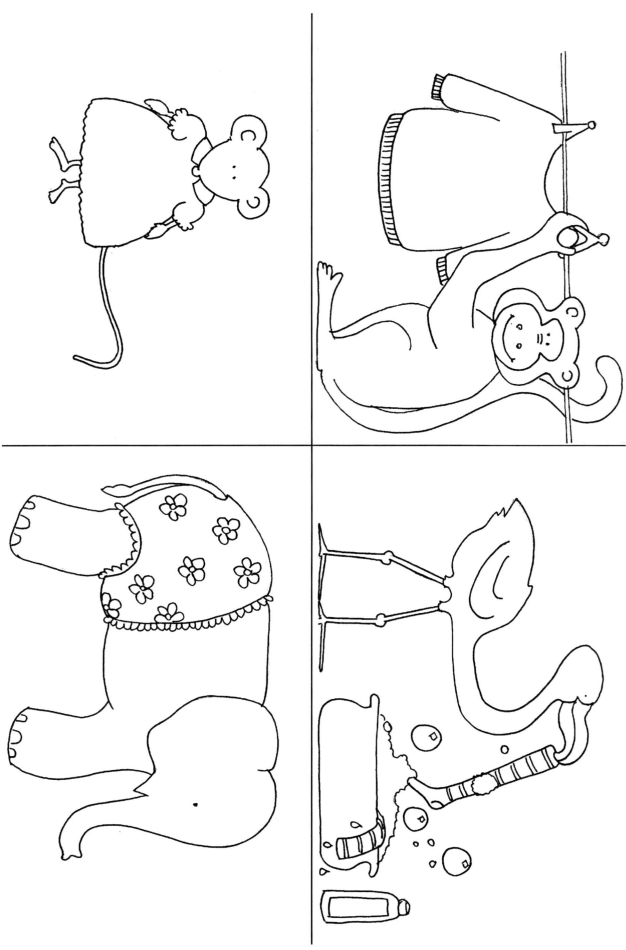

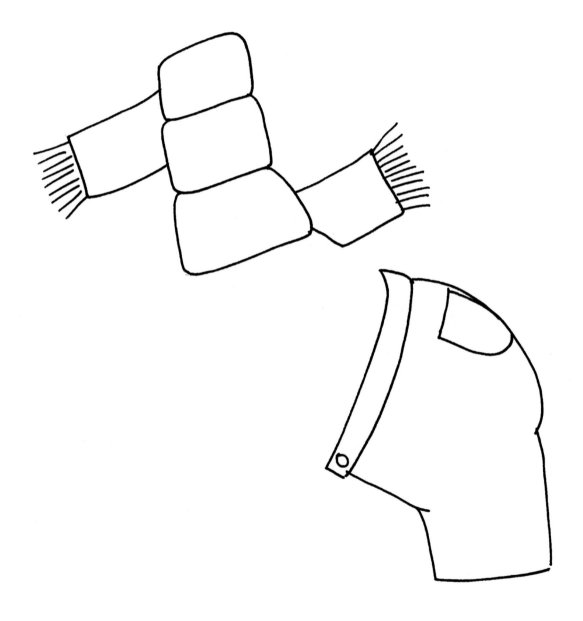

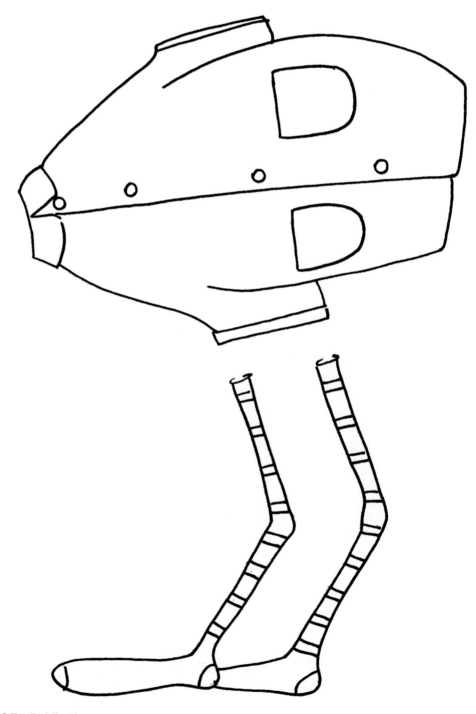

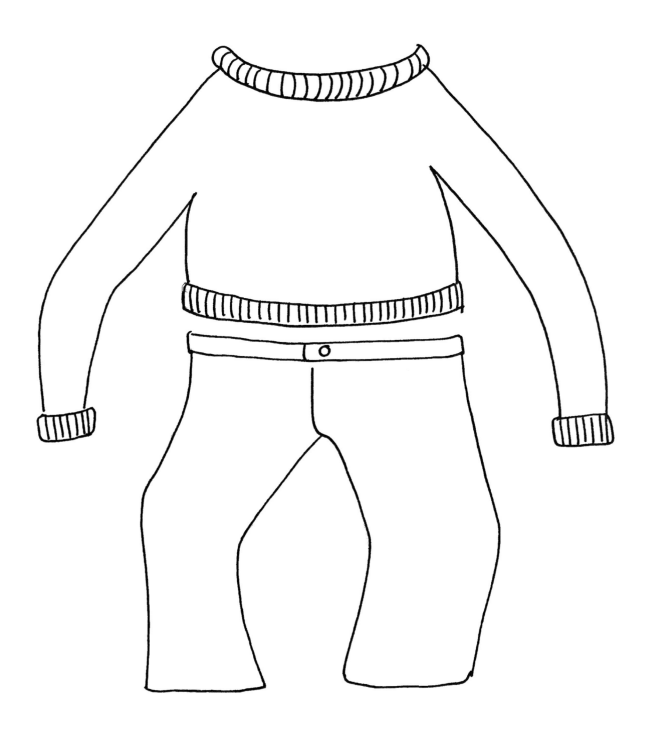

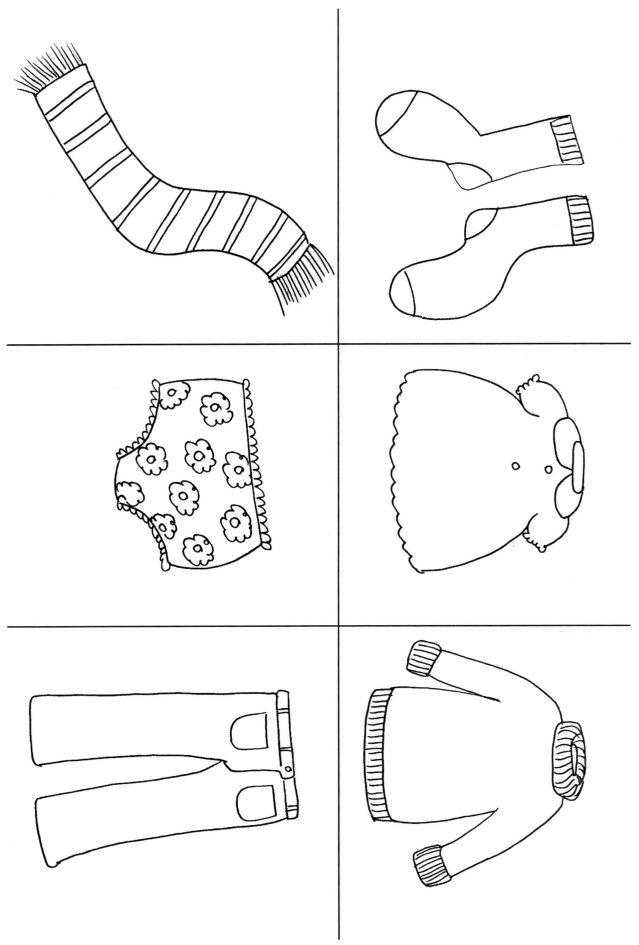

129

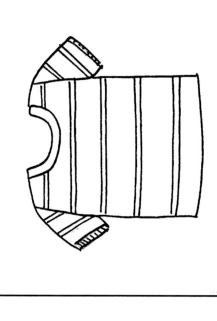

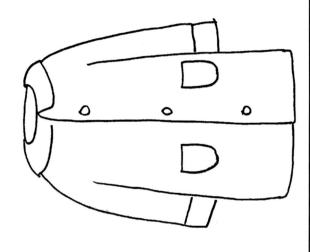

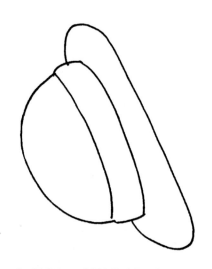

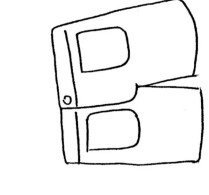

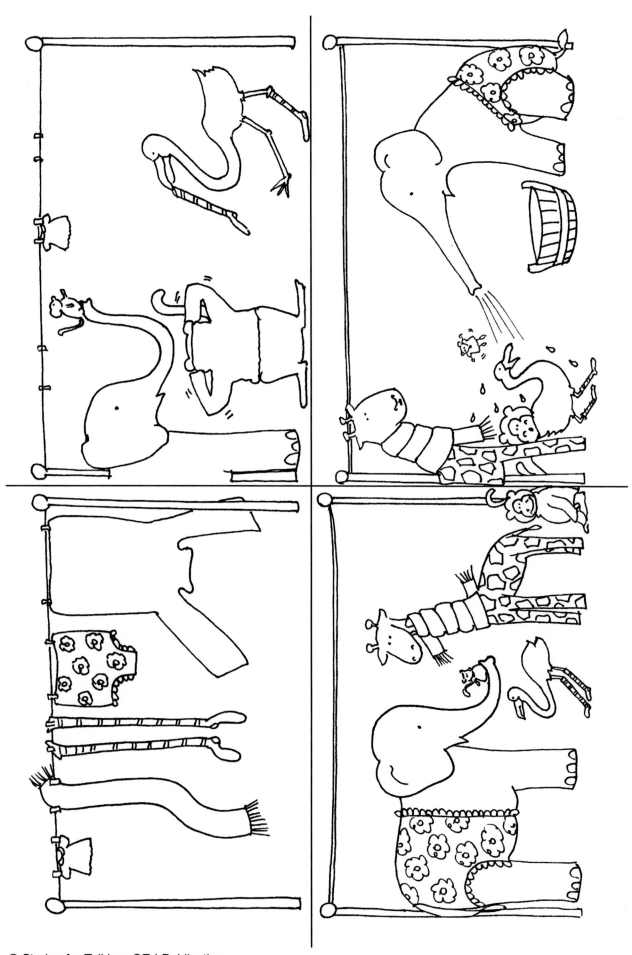

The Enormous Turnip

Section index

The Enormous Turnip

Section index continued

The Enormous Turnip

Level 1 – Introducing vocabulary

Topic category	My family and pets; growing
Nouns (object words) – basic level	man woman/lady boy girl baby cat dog mouse seeds turnip
Notes	While this story is about a turnip and growth, the characters lend themselves nicely to a topic on people names, families and pets, as well as covering aspects of gardening and growth. For this reason, this story is a little different from others used in this approach, as it covers two themes, and the vocabulary chosen reflects this dual theme. 'Baby' has been added to make up the 'set' of people names. 'Seeds' and 'turnip' do not relate to the people/family/pets theme, but have been chosen as they are central to the theme of the book.
Verbs (action words)	planting watering digging pulling eating
	These are the main verbs mentioned in the book. They relate more to the 'turnip' vocabulary than the 'people' vocabulary chosen. 'Digging' has been added as it is a tangible verb which young children can relate to.
Concepts	**young** **old**
Notes	These concepts are not typical early concepts to introduce. However, these words relate to the topic of people and families and the idea of growth. If the children you are working with at Level 1 have only very limited language, you may wish to omit the activities covering these concepts.
Parts of a whole vocabulary	The text in this story is limited and short, and no other harder vocabulary is covered. If desired, you could develop work on harder vocabulary by exploring 'parts of a plant', for example: **seed** **flower** **roots** **bud** **leaf** **pollen** **petal** **stalk** Alternatively, you could introduce additional 'family' vocabulary: **brother** **aunty** **grandad** **daddy** **sister** **cousin** **uncle** **granny**

Story: The Enormous Turnip

Topic: My family and pets; growing

**My family and pets
Growing**

Five verbs
planting, watering,
digging, pulling, eating

Ten nouns
man, woman/lady, boy,
girl, baby, cat, dog,
mouse, seeds, turnip

Two concepts
young, old

Parts of a whole/harder vocabulary

seed, flower, roots, bud,
leaf, petal, stalk, pollen

or

brother, sister, aunty,
uncle, cousin, gran,
grandad, Mum, Dad

Weekly plan for Level 1 – Introducing vocabulary

Monday	
Focus	**Understanding object words**
What you need	A packet of seeds and a turnip; photos/pictures of a 'man', 'lady', 'boy', 'girl', 'baby', 'cat', 'dog' and 'mouse' (you could cut these out from a magazine); a large photo album – preferably one with peel back plastic covers to put photos underneath.
Activity 1	Read the story and show the children the seeds and turnip at the appropriate point in the story, to reinforce learning and understanding of these words.
Activity 2	Lay out the photos/pictures on the floor. Explain that you want to put them in a special photo album. Ask each child to find you one of the people or pets, and help you stick it in the album, for example: 'Callum, put the baby in the photo album'; 'Lizzie, put the cat in the photo album'.
Notes	Remember, each day when you read the story you will be pointing out and emphasising all of the key vocabulary as it appears in the story and pictures. All of the vocabulary is therefore mentioned each day, but on certain days the activities and resources you use will particularly focus on one of the different word classes.
Tuesday	
Focus	**Naming object words**
What you need	Photos of people (as used on Monday); a 'feely' bag; photo album.
Activity 1	Read the story. Leave a pause to see if the children can name the people/animal characters in the book as you get to each page.
Activity 2	Put the photos in the feely bag. Pass the bag around and each child has a turn to label the person/animal, for example: 'It's a lady' – and then stick it in the album.

Weekly plan for Level 1 (continued)	
Wednesday	
Focus	**Understanding verbs (action words)**
What you need	A packet of seeds; a spade and watering can for each child; a turnip.
Activity 1	Read the story. Give each child a seed, a spade and a watering can. Pause at each stage in the 'growing' phase of the story. Act out each action word with the children, for example: 'Digging', 'Planting', 'Watering'. At the end of the story, get them all to join together in a long line and pretend to pull the turnip up. If possible, using a digital camera, take photos of the children 'planting', 'watering', 'pulling' and 'digging'. *You need to develop these photos ready for tomorrow's activity.*
Thursday	
Focus	**Naming verbs (action words)**
What you need	Photos of children from Wednesday; photo album.
Activity 1	Read the story. Pause at each action word and see if the children can tell you what the man/people are doing, for example: 'planting', 'watering' and so on.
Activity 2	Put the photographs you took the day before face down, or hold them face down like a hand of cards. Ask each child in turn to choose a picture. She/he must then guess what the child is doing, such as 'digging', before sticking it in the photo album. The album could then be left out in the nursery to stimulate further interest and discussion.
Friday	
Focus	**Understanding and naming concepts**
What you need	Feely bag; pictures/photos from magazines of 'old' and 'young' people (choose pictures where the contrast is very obvious). Plan this in advance as pictures of elderly people are not very common in catalogues/magazines.
Activity 1	Read the story. Emphasise the idea that the man and lady are 'old' and the boy and girl are 'young'.
Activity 2	Lay out two hoops. Put a photo of an old person in one and a young person in the other. Explain this to the children. Pass the feely bag containing a mixture of pictures, around the group. Each child has a turn to take a picture and decide if it goes with the 'old' people or the 'young' people. Continue to emphasise the concepts as they sort out the pictures.
Parent/carer activity	Ask parents/carers to look through photographs of the child's family and friends. Encourage the parents/carers to share with the child who is a lady/man/boy/girl/baby and point out people who look 'young' and 'old'.

Weekly plan for Level 2a – Building phrases and sentences – two words together	*The Enormous Turnip*
Monday	
Focus	**Modelling two word phrases** – combinations of a noun (a person or animal) and a verb, for example 'boy pulling'.
What you need	Only the book is required for this.
Activity 1	Read the story. Model all of the two word phrases as you come across them in the story, for example: 'man planting'; 'man watering'; 'boy pulling'; 'girl eating' On the pages where it is repetitive, get the children to join in with you to make it more fun.
Tuesday	
Focus	**Two key word comprehension**
What you need	Two seed trays – one with soil only, and one with a planted turnip; seeds; a watering can; a spade/trowel; a plastic sheet (if storytime is in a carpeted area); a dog/cat soft toy; digital camera (very important).
Activity 1	Read the story, but more briefly on this occasion.
Activity 2	Play, 'Simon Says', but using the toy dog/cat. Choose children from the group at random and make 'dog' give a direction. For example: 'Dog says . . . Michael dig' or 'Seena water', 'Ben plant' or 'Rona pull' (use the 5 verbs chosen to make up the directions). Michael (or whoever is chosen) must listen for his/her name and then the action, and then perform the action with the gardening props. Take a photo of each child doing their action, using a digital camera. It is important to choose children randomly from the group so that they have to listen carefully for their name as well as the action they must perform – this way there are two key words in each instruction. You will need to print the photos ready for tomorrow's activity.
Wednesday	
Focus	**Expressive language activity – two words together**
What you need	Yesterday's photos; a photo album, preferably one with sticky plastic sheets that cover the photos.
Activity 1	Read the story.
Activity 2	Hold out the photos from yesterday, like pack of cards, or place them face down on the floor. Give each child a turn to choose a photo and say what is happening in it, for example, 'Seena watering'. They then show it and give it to that child and then Seena sticks it in the photo album.

Weekly plan for Level 2a (continued)

Thursday	
Focus	**Expressive language activity – two words together**
What you need	Lotto games (photocopy pages 159-160). Photocopy each twice – leave one sheet whole and cut the other one up to make lotto games); a toy dog; a toy cat.
Activity 1	Read the story.
Activity 2	Play lotto. Give the dog and cat a lotto baseboard each. Place the lotto cards face down on the carpet. The children take a turn each at choosing a card and describing the picture, for example: 'Lady digging' or 'Mouse eating'. They can then match it on the appropriate baseboard. See whether the children helped the dog or the cat to win!
Friday	
Focus	**Expressive language activity – two words together**
What you need	A turnip; watering can (empty); a spade.
Activity 1	Before you begin to read the story, choose a child to 'help'. Ask him/her to stand next to you as you read and their job is to choose another child to act out the action shown on that page. For example, where the book shows a man digging, the child might say 'Peter dig'. Peter then acts it out and then is the next person to stand next to you and to give a direction to another child. When you get to the pulling bit of the story, keep the children at the front and act it out. Each child must choose a friend for the next character, just like in 'The dog wants a bone'. For example John is the 'man' who has to call to the lady. **You:** 'John, who is going to be the 'lady'? **John:** 'Er . . Emma'. **You:** 'OK, tell Emma what to do'. **John:** 'Emma pull'. Emma joins John at the front and helps him pull the turnip. Then Emma chooses another child to be the 'boy' and so on.
Parent/carer activity	Lotto game as played on Thursday (photocopy pages 159-160 twice).

Weekly plan for Level 2b – Building phrases and sentences – three words together	*The Enormous Turnip*

Notes	These activities are for children who use two or three word phrases and have a good vocabulary for basic objects. The following activities are to elicit three word sentences, for example: subject/person + action word + object word They range from easier repetitive sentences, to creating more difficult, varied sentences at the end of the week.
Monday	
Focus	**Expressive language activity – three words together**
What you need	A small amount of cooked carrot, turnip and potato; a spoon and plate for each child; a soft toy cat and dog. Perhaps the children could prepare and cook the vegetables with you earlier in the day. If you do this, remember to take photos of the children preparing the vegetables – they make excellent resources for the children to talk about.
Activity 1	Read the story.
Activity 2	Have a vegetable tasting session. Encourage each child to try all three vegetables. Next, go around the group and ask each child to say 'I like . . .' You may need to model this first – give yourself, the cat and the dog a vegetable on a plate: **You:** 'I like carrots'. **Dog says:**'I like turnips'. **Cat says:** 'I like potatoes' **You:** 'Anna, what do you like?' **Anna:** 'Carrots' **You:** 'Oh, so you say 'I like carrots''.
Tuesday	
Focus	**Three key word comprehension**
What you need	Some raw, uncooked potatoes, carrots and pieces of turnip.
Activity 1	Read the story.
Activity 2	Ask each child to remember which vegetable they liked yesterday (if they say 'none', ask them to choose the one they really did not like). Then get each child to take the vegetable they liked/hated and keep it in front of them. Each child has a turn to choose a friend. Check whether the friend liked or disliked the vegetable. The child whose turn it is has to construct a sentence. For example: 'Abigail likes potato' or 'Abigail (does) not like potato' (the word 'does' is in brackets as it is highly likely that a child at this level of language will omit it and say 'Abigail not like potato'. This is fine – do not insist they say 'does' in the sentence). Let each child have a turn choosing a friend to comment on whether they liked/did not like their vegetable. Model this activity first.

Weekly plan for Level 2b (continued)

Wednesday	
Focus	**Expressive language activity – building simple sentences**
What you need	Raw vegetables (as used on Tuesday); soft toy cat and dog; one dog bowl and one cat bowl.
Activity 1	Read the story.
Activity 2	Message-giving activity. Give the cat and dog a bowl each and put the vegetables in the centre of the group. Let the children take it in turns to give a message to a friend about feeding the pets. For example: 'John, give the dog a carrot'. John does this, and then says 'dog eating carrot'. You will need to model these sentences first. Make sure each child gets a turn at being a message-giver, and a friend.
Thursday	
Focus	**Three key word comprehension**
What you need	Sentence building pictures (photocopy pages 161-162); pictures of cats' and dogs' bowls (photocopy pages 150-151); fish and bones pictures (photocopy page 152); toy cat and dog.
Activity 1	Read the story.
Activity 2	Lay out the sentence-building cards face up, across the floor. Hide the fish and bones, one under each picture card. Ask each child to find the picture you describe. For example: 'Sarah, find a <u>boy</u> <u>digging</u> a <u>turnip</u>'; 'Mark, find a <u>man</u> <u>watering</u> the <u>flowers</u>'. When the child finds the picture, they pick it up, find the bone/fish and give it to the dog/cat. Either the dog or cat is the winner – whichever has their bowl filled first. It is important that, after each turn, the picture card is placed back on the carpet with the others. If not the comprehension activity will become easier for each child as the choices are removed.

Weekly plan for Level 2b (continued)

Friday	
Focus	**Building three word sentences**
What you need	Sentence building pictures (as on Thursday); pictures of cats' and dogs' bowls (as on Thursday); fish and bones picures (as on Thursday); toy cat and dog.
Activity 1	Read the story.
Activity 2	Play 'Feed-me Pets game'. Give the cat the card you have photocopied of the cat's bowl and the dog the dog's bowl. Lay the sentence-building pictures out on the floor, face down this time and hide either a 'bones' or a 'fish' picture underneath each picture card. Let each child take a turn to choose a picture card. They should have either a bone or a fish underneath, which they place in the dog or cat bowl, depending on what they find. The child then looks at the picture card and makes up a sentence to describe it. For example: 'The girl's watering the flowers'; 'The boy's pulling the turnip'. You may need to help the child build this sentence. If they only say one or two words, prompt them to use parts of the picture that they did not mention and then put the whole sentence together. For example: **Child:** 'Water flowers'. **You:** 'Yes that's right, watering the flowers. Who is this?' **Child:** 'Girl'. **You:** 'That's right, girl watering the flowers. Can you say it?' Another approach could be like this: **Child:** 'Water flowers'. **You:** 'Yes, watering flowers. Is it a <u>boy</u> watering flowers or a <u>girl</u> watering flowers?'
Parent/carer activity	Photocopy the sentence-building pictures (page 161-162, each page twice) to make into a pairs game.

Weekly plan for Level 3 – Narrative	*The Enormous Turnip*
Notes	The aim of this level is to give children an opportunity to experiment with creative story telling, develop combinations of two, three or more sentences, and develop an understanding and use of sequencing. This level is not suitable for children who have only recently begun to combine words in sentences.
Monday	
Focus	**Sequencing – matching pictures**
What you need	Sequencing pictures (photocopy page 157-158).
Activity 1	Read the story.
Activity 2	Go back through the story and match the sequencing pictures to the corresponding part of the story. This will enable the children to lay out the sequencing cards in order.
Activity 3	Re-tell the story (in brief) from the sequencing strip of pictures.
Tuesday	
Focus	**Sequencing – using memory**
What you need	Sequencing pictures (as on Monday).
Activity 1	Read the story.
Activity 2	Without using the book, see if the children can sequence the pictures in order. Re-tell the story from the sequencing strip.

Wednesday	
Focus	**Sequencing – acting out the story**
What you need	A spade, watering can, pretend seeds (you could use beads for example); a large turnip.
Activity 1	Read the story.
Activity 2	Act out the story with the children. Start them off: 'There was an old man', (choose a child to be the old man) 'who planted some turnip seeds – Joshua, can you pretend to plant seeds. What happened next?' After each stage ask the children to tell you what happened next. Use the pictures from the book to prompt if the children have forgotten. Try to make sure each child has a turn at saying what happened next. Encourage some turn-taking rather than allowing the most vocal and confident ones to dominate the activity. Next, ask each child to choose who the next character will be, just like in 'The Farmer Needs a Wife' game. Encourage the children to use the language of the book when asking for their friend. For example: **You:** 'Who do you want to be the little boy?' **Children:** 'Fred'. **You:** 'Okay, Fred's the little boy. What do you say to him?' **Children:** 'Little boy – we can't pull up this enormous turnip, come and help us'. Help the children form a long line, pretending to pull up and then eat the enormous turnip.
Thursday	
Focus	**Sequencing – retelling the story**
What you need	Pictures of objects and characters (photocopy pages 153-154 and colour them in if you have time); a washing line/string, hung up; clothes pegs (springy type).
Activity 1	**Don't** read the story!
Activity 2	Lay out the pictures in front of the children. Re-tell the story together using the pictures, and clipping them onto the washing line as you go along. Start off the story – clip the man and his seeds to the line, then ask the children: 'What happened next?' Give each child a turn to find the next object/character required, peg it on the line and tell the next part of the story. Use the story book to prompt if the children have trouble remembering what happens next.

Weekly plan for Level 3 (continued)

Friday	
Focus	**Creating a new story**
What you need	Pictures (as used yesterday) but also add extra pictures (photocopy and colour pages 155 and 156); a washing line and pegs.
Activity 1	**Don't read the story!** Today is creative day for making up a new story.
Activity 2	Lay out all the pictures on the floor. Explain to the children that you are making up a new story and so there are lots of new pictures to choose and use to tell a story. Help begin the story. Start with a different character to give the children some new ideas. Ask the children to take turns to choose any of the pictures, add them to the washing line and add a new part to the story. Help come up with an ending to the story once each child has had a turn. Do not worry if the children go off at a tangent, become repetitive, don't make logical suggestions or make up an exciting story. Initially, it is just about the children having an opportunity to be creative, expressing basic ideas and learning to take turns at being the storyteller.
Parent/carer activity	Photocopy the sequencing strip for The Enormous Turnip on pages 157 and 158. Send this home for the children to practise sequencing and telling the story.

Enormous Turnip – generalising language and skills within the EYFS	
Notes	Generalising the language and skills taught throughout other activities in the EYFS gives essential opportunities for **repetition** and **functional** use of language to improve social skills and confidence. Here are some examples of activities to build on the language used in *The Enormous Turnip*. Under each activity heading are just some possible Focuses of Development within the Early Years Foundation Stage.
Sand tray Personal, Social and Emotional Development – Self-care	Compost, spades, plant pots, pretend seeds such as beads, plastic flowers etc.
In the garden Knowledge and Understanding of the World – Time	Make a garden area or have large tubs/containers available to do digging, watering etc in free play. Plant seeds such as cress, sunflowers.
Outdoor games Communication, Language and Literacy – Language for Thinking	Pulling games such as tug of war; pulling each other in trolleys/carts – you comment on their play using the action word 'pulling'.
Jigsaws Problem Solving, Reasoning and Numeracy – Shape, Space and Measures	Growth sequencing puzzles.
Making and Creating Creative Development – Exploring Media and Materials	Make pictures or collages using a variety of different kinds of seeds.
Painting Creative Development – Exploring Media and Materials	Try printing images onto paper using various vegetables including turnips.
Snack time Personal, Social and Emotional Development – Self-care	Use vegetables such as carrot sticks; make vegetable soup. Allow the children to help to chop up the vegetables and watch the cooking process and then try it for snack.
Home corner Personal, Social and Emotional Development – Self-care	Have real vegetables available to 'cook' and play with such as turnips, carrots, potatoes, peas in their pods and so on.
Small world play Communication, Language and Literacy – Language for Thinking	Get together characters from the story – a man, lady, boy, girl, baby, dog, cat available in the dolls house so that they can re-enact the story.
Books Communication, Language and Literacy – Reading	Use photo albums with photos/pictures of young and old people including boys, girls, men, ladies, and babies and any other pictures associated with the story.
Interactive displays Personal, Social and Emotional Development – Sense of Community	Cut out pictures of different people from magazines/ catalogues and laminate. The children can stick the pictures in different 'family' groupings in a basic outline of a house.

Photocopiable Resources
for
The Enormous Turnip

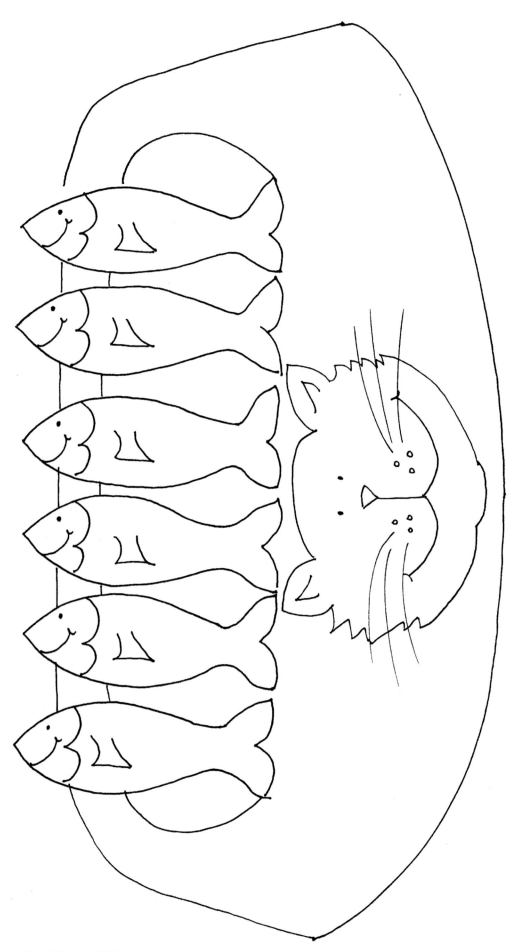

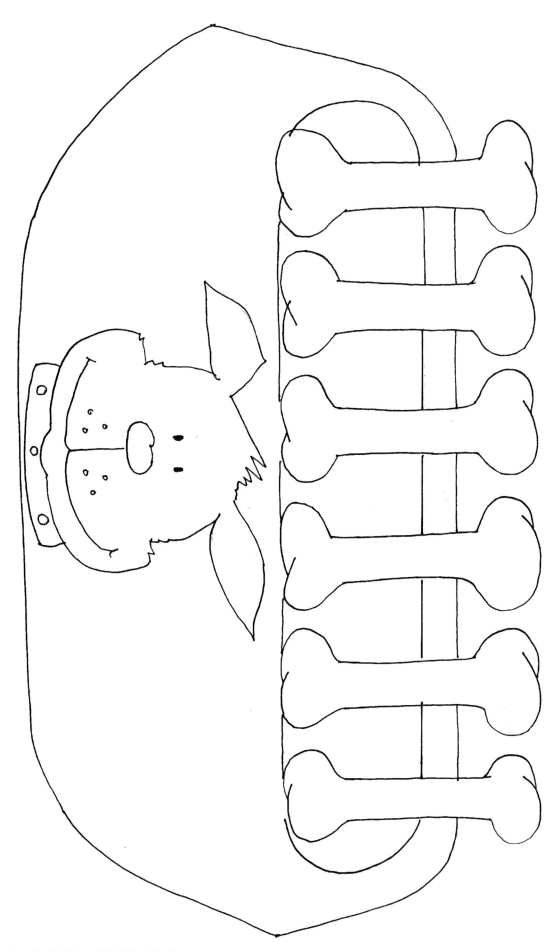

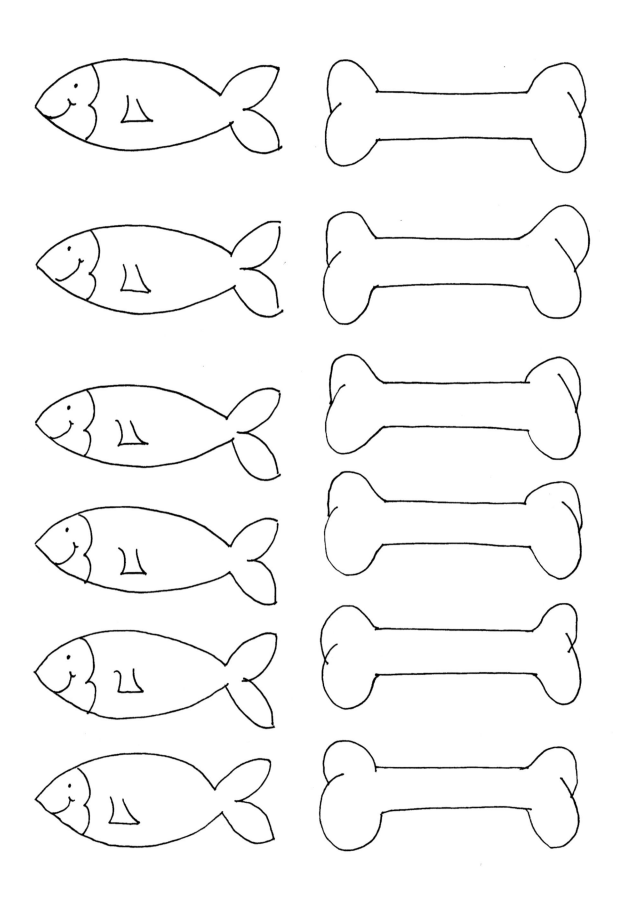

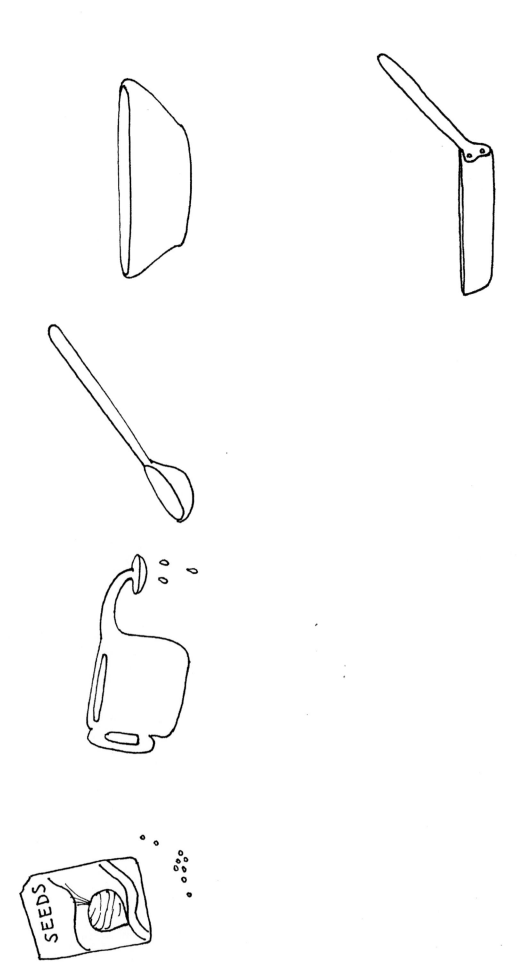

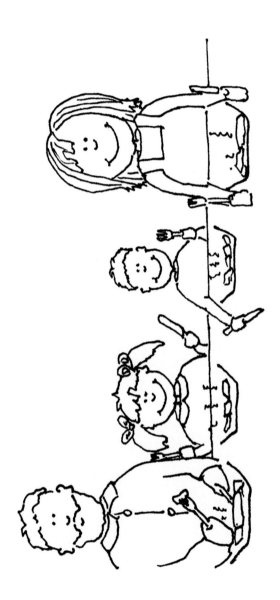

Walking through the Jungle

by Julie Lacome

Section index

Walking through the Jungle

Section index continued

Walking through the Jungle

Level 1 – Introducing vocabulary

Topic category	Jungle animals
Nouns (object words) – basic level	**snake** **elephant** **monkey** **tiger** **lion** **crocodile** **zebra** **hippo** **camel** **giraffe**
Notes	The first six words are featured in the book. The other four words have been added to make up the set of 10 object words. You can change these if you have toy plastic animals for other jungle animals instead. Parrot and flamingo are pictured in the book, but are not commented on in the text. These words are less familiar and so have not been chosen in the core list of 10 object words. If you wish, you could comment on them and label them in passing as you are reading the book.
Verbs (action words)	**walking** **running** **creeping (crawling)** **leaping (jumping)** **wading (splashing)** Five of the six verbs mentioned in the book have been chosen based on ability to act them out, as well as their frequency of use. Some verbs have been changed to more common everyday words, which have similar meanings. For example, 'leaping' has been changed to 'jumping', as we are far more likely to talk about 'jumping' to a three year-old child. When reading, either change the words (so read 'jumping' instead of 'leaping') or read the text as it is, but comment on the picture saying 'Look, he's leaping and jumping', adding and stressing the more familiar verb word.
Concepts	**noisy** **quiet**
Notes	These concepts are not mentioned in the book, but neither are any others. However, there is a lot of emphasis on listening throughout the story. For example: 'I can hear a noise' and the noises that the animals make. And so concepts that relate to listening and noise fit well here.
Parts of a whole vocabulary	Remember, this is only taught to children who have a good grasp of the basic vocabulary and are able to both understand and label (say) the basic words listed earlier. In this story, the harder bird words and jungle environment words are chosen as harder vocabulary. **bird** **trees** **water** **grass** **parrot** **leaves** **mud** **flamingo** **flowers** **swamp**

Story: Walking through the jungle

Topic: Jungle animals

Jungle animals

Five verbs
walking, crawling,
jumping, splashing,
running

Ten nouns
snake, elephant, monkey,
tiger, lion, crocodile, zebra,
hippo, camel, giraffe

Two concepts
noisy, quiet

Parts of a whole/harder vocabulary

bird, parrot, flamingo,
trees, leaves, flowers,
water, mud, swamp, grass

Weekly plan for Level 1 – Introducing vocabulary	*Walking through the Jungle*
Monday	
Focus	**Understanding object words**
What you need	Plastic toy animals to represent your 10 object words; a mini 'jungle' environment (see activities for generalising language and skills within the EYFS on page 176). You could use a water tray with twigs to represent trees, a bowl of water as the swamp and add some moss and flowers (rather like how you might make an Easter garden).
Activity 1	Read the story.
Activity 2	Put the animals out in front of the children and explain they want to go and live in the jungle. Encourage each child in turn to listen and find a jungle animal. For example: 'Lucy, find the elephant' (Lucy picks up the elephant). 'Well done, can you put it in the jungle now?' If a child is struggling to understand and cannot cope with scanning across all 10 animals, you should reduce the choice to just two or three and give the instruction again.
Notes	Remember, each day when you read the story you will be pointing out and emphasising all of the key vocabulary as it appears in the story and pictures. All of the vocabulary is therefore mentioned each day, but on certain days the activities and resources you use will particularly focus on one of the different word classes.
Tuesday	
Focus	**Naming object words (the animals)**
What you need	Plastic toy animals that correspond with your 10 object words; a 'feely' bag (an interesting looking bag or box); the mini jungle environment used on Monday.
Activity 1	Read the story.
Activity 2	Pass the feely bag around the group. Give each child a turn to pull out an animal, name it and place it in the 'jungle'. If a child is struggling to name an animal, offer him/her a choice. For example: Diego pulls out giraffe and either says nothing or gives the wrong answer. You say 'Is it a monkey or a giraffe?'

Weekly plan for Level 1 (continued)

Walking through the Jungle

Wednesday	
Focus	**Understanding verbs (action words)**
What you need	Animal masks (photocopy pages 178-183) colour these in and cut out and laminate to use as masks
Activity 1	Read the story. Try to make this a very active storytime where both you and the children act out the action words (such as 'crawling', 'running', 'splashing') during the telling of the story.
Activity 2	Let each child take a turn to choose a mask to wear. Ask them to perform an action, for example: 'Can you <u>run</u> like a lion?'; 'Can you <u>walk</u> like an elephant?'; 'Can you <u>splash</u> like a hippo?'
Thursday	
Focus	**Naming verbs (action words)**
What you need	Animal masks (as used on Thursday).
Activity 1	Read the story. Once again act out the verbs together as a group during the telling of the story.
Activity 2	Play the 'Simon says' game. Give each child a turn to choose a mask. Choose another child to tell the masked child what to do, for example: 'Simon says . . . crawl like a snake'. Make sure each child has a turn at wearing a mask and acting out an action, as well as being the 'teacher' to give an instruction.
Friday	
Focus	**Understanding and naming concepts**
What you need	A tape of animal noises of the six featured in the book – some should be noisy and others quiet. (You will need to prepare this in advance - if you are unable to make a tape, you will need to make loud/quiet animal noises during the group session. However, a tape and tape player always adds more interest and keeps children's attention and listening/anticipation more easily.)
Activity 1	Read the story.
Activity 2	Ask the children to listen carefully to the loud or quiet animal noises and say if the noise is 'loud' or 'quiet'.
Parent/carer activity	Photocopy and enlarge the jungle scene (page 184) and animals (page 185). Give these to the children and parents/carers to talk about, cut out and stick on jungle scene.

Weekly plan for Level 2a – Building phrases and sentences – two words together

Monday	
Focus	**Modelling two word phrases** – combinations of a noun (a person or animal) and a verb, for example 'boy pulling'.
What you need	Only the book is required for this.
Activity 1	Read the story. Model all of the two word phrases as you come across them in the story, for example: 'boy walking'; 'boy splashing'; 'snake looking'; 'monkey looking'; 'lion running'; 'monkey swinging'.
Tuesday	
Focus	**Two key word comprehension**
What you need	Plastic toy animals; toy food.
Activity 1	Read the story.
Activity 2	Explain that in the story, all the animals are looking for their dinner. Ask the children to listen carefully to find out what food each animal wants. Give each child a turn to listen and follow an instruction. For example: 'Sophie, give <u>monkey</u> a <u>cake</u>'; 'Dylan, give <u>crocodile</u> an <u>apple</u>'.
Wednesday	
Focus	**Expressive language activity – putting two words together**
What you need	Plastic toy animals; toy food.
Activity 1	Read the story.
Activity 2	Lay the food and animals out for the children to see. Explain that the children are going to take turns to be the 'teacher' today. Ask the 'teacher' to choose a friend to give a message to. For example: **You:** 'Chloe, who will you choose?' **Chloe:** 'Jane'. **You:** 'Okay, Jane, are you listening to Chloe's message?' **Jane:** 'Yes'. **Chloe:** 'Give snake a banana'. The 'teacher' may need help choosing an animal and then an item of food, and then putting the two words into a phrase. The other child may need support listening to the message – you may need to repeat it, particularly if the 'teacher' has unclear speech.

Weekly plan for Level 2a (continued)	*Walking through the Jungle*
Thursday	
Focus	**Two key word comprehension**
What you need	Animal masks (photocopy pages 178-183); colour and prepare as masks).
Activity 1	Read the story.
Activity 2	Lay out the masks on the floor. Encourage each child to take a turn to listen to an instruction given by you, find a mask, and then act it out. For example: 'George, can you be a crocodile crawling?'; 'Abigail, can you be a lion splashing?' The child must listen carefully to know which animal mask to pick up and wear, and then which action to perform.
Friday	
Focus	**Expressive language activity – putting two words together**
What you need	Animal masks (as used on Thursday).
Activity 1	Read the story.
Activity 2	Do the same activity as yesterday, but this time each child has a turn to be the 'teacher' and give a message to their chosen partner/friend. As before, some children may need support to build up the two word phrase, first choosing an animal and then thinking of an action for it to perform.
Parent/carer activity	Photocopy page 185 twice to make a lotto game. Parents/carers can talk about the pictures, modelling and encouraging the child to make two word phrases, such as 'lion running' and 'crocodile splashing'.

Weekly plan for Level 2b – Building phrases and sentences – three words together	*Walking through the Jungle*
Notes	These activities are for children who use two or three word phrases and have a good vocabulary for basic objects. The following activities are to elicit three word sentences, for example: subject/person + action word + object word They range from easier repetitive sentences, to creating more difficult, varied sentences at the end of the week.
Monday	
Focus	**Three key word comprehension**
What you need	Toy/plastic animals; toy food.
Activity 1	Read the story.
Activity 2	Explain that in the story all the animals are looking for their dinner. Tell the children that they need to listen to see what each animal wants. For example: 'Mohammed, give tiger a banana and some bread'; 'Jonathan, give elephant a sausage and a carrot'.
Tuesday	
Focus	**Expressive language activity – three word sentences**
What you need	Toy/plastic animals; toy food.
Activity 1	Read the story.
Activity 2	Do the same activity as yesterday, but today give each child a turn to be the 'teacher' and choose another child to give a message to. Help the 'teacher' choose an animal and two pieces of food, then build a sentence using those words, to make up their message. For example: 'Give the <u>lion</u> an <u>apple</u> and a <u>sausage</u>'. The child listening to the message may need you to repeat it again, after the 'teacher' has given the message.
Wednesday	
Focus	**Expressive language activity – three word sentences**
What you need	Toy/plastic animals; 'feely' bag or box; jungle environment.
Activity 1	Read the story pointing out the different types of jungle habitat such as trees, grass, mud and water.
Activity 2	Ask each child to take a turn to take an animal out of the feely bag. Help them decide where to put it (give them a choice, such as 'trees or water?') and then help the child decode what the animal can do, for example, 'splash or run?'. Next, model the end sentence. For example: 'So you want <u>monkey</u> <u>splashing</u> in the <u>water</u>'.

Weekly plan for Level 2b (continued)	
<td colspan="1" align="center">**Thursday**</td>	
Focus	**Building three word sentences**
What you need	Toy animals; 'feely' bag; mini-jungle environment.
Activity 1	Read the story.
Activity 2	Repeat the same activity as Wednesday. Hopefully the children will need a few less prompts from you and may begin putting the three word sentence together by themselves.
<td colspan="1" align="center">**Friday**</td>	
Focus	**Building three word sentences**
What you need	Toy animals; 'feely' bag; mini-jungle environment.
Activity 1	Read the story.
Activity 2	If the children have become quite competent at building three word sentences, you can adapt Thursday's activity into a message giving game. Do not use a feely bag this time – instead put the animals on the floor near the jungle environment. Choose one child to be the 'teacher' who will give a message to a friend. For example: 'Johnny, make <u>lion</u> <u>run</u> in the <u>mud</u>'. If the children are still struggling to build three word sentences and are still heavily reliant on your support and prompts, repeat the same activity as on Wednesday and Thursday.
Parent/carer activity	Photocopy the jungle habitat on page 184 and the animals on page 185. Encourage parents/carers to talk about the pictures with their child, whilst cutting and sticking the animals onto the jungle picture and making sentences such as 'Crocodile splashing in the water'.

Weekly plan for Level 3 – Narrative	*Walking through the Jungle*
Notes	The aim of this level is to give children an opportunity to experiment with creative story telling, develop combinations of two, three or more sentences, and develop an understanding and use of sequencing. This level is not suitable for children who have only recently begun to combine words in sentences.
Monday	
Focus	**Sequencing – matching pictures**
What you need	Sequencing pictures (photocopy pages 186-188).
Activity 1	Read the story.
Activity 2	Go back through the story and match the sequencing pictures to the corresponding part of the story.
Activity 3	Re-tell the story (in brief) from the sequencing strip of pictures. Use cue-cards and 'who?', 'where?', and 'what happened?' to prompt.
Tuesday	
Focus	**Sequencing – using memory**
What you need	Sequencing pictures (as on Monday).
Activity 1	Read the story.
Activity 2	Recall the story together and put sequence cards in the correct order. If the children are struggling to work out which one goes next, go back to the book and check by matching.
Wednesday	
Focus	**Sequencing – retelling the story with toys**
What you need	A toy figure of a boy; toy animals to represent the animals shown in the book.
Activity 1	Read the story.
Activity 2	Give each child an animal. Use the toys to re-tell the story together.

Weekly plan for Level 3 (continued)	*Walking through the Jungle*
Thursday	
Focus	**Creating a new story**
What you need	A toy figure of a boy and animals as yesterday. Jungle environment is preferable e.g. Easter garden style, jungle in sand/water tray, with twigs/branches for trees, bowl of water for pond, soil for mud, flowers etc.
Activity 1	**Don't** read the story! Today, you will make up a story which involves the same animals/characters. Keep it simple and short. Each child has an animal to hold – when the child hears you talk about that animal in your story, they must listen and make it do as you are saying.
Friday	
Focus	**Creating a new story**
What you need	A toy figure of a boy; toy animals to represent the animals shown in the book; mini-jungle environment.
Activity 1	**Don't** read the story! Today you and the children will make up a story together. Give each child an animal and encourage them to take it in turns to add a line or two (or an idea) to develop a story together as a group. You will need to start the story off, and later you may need to prompt the children with simple questions such as 'What happened?' and '<u>Where</u> did we go?', to give ideas to the children. Once every child has had an opportunity to add something to the story you can create a suitable ending.
Parent/carer activity	Photocopy the sequencing pictures (pages 186-188) for the children to practise sequencing the pictures and re-telling the story.

Walking through the Jungle – generalising language and skills within the EYFS	
Notes	Generalising the language and skills taught throughout other activities in the EYFS gives essential opportunities for **repetition** and **functional** use of language to improve social skills and confidence. Here are some examples of activities to build on the language used in *Walking through the Jungle*. Under each activity heading are just some possible Focuses of Development within the Early Years Foundation Stage.
Water/sand tray Creative Development – Being Creative	Make a jungle environment, like a traditional Easter garden, using moss, flowers, trees with twigs/branches/leaves, water in a dish, mud and so on. Put plastic jungle animals in the mini-jungle to create a realistic small world play environment. Other small word play activities could be around a zoo environment, such as Playmobile zoo.
Designing and making Creative Development – Developing Imagination and Imaginative Play	Make animal masks in the creative area that the children can wear to play outdoors, pretending to be animals. Lots of commentary using action words will be very beneficial. Make animal finger puppets.
Home corner and role play	Provide lots of soft toys of jungle animals. Encourage the children to make them their tea.
Outdoor play Communication, Language and Literacy – Language for Thinking	Play 'Simon says' using the verb words targeted in this story Play 'What's the time Mr Wolf?' but change the game to 'What's for dinner, Mr Crocodile?' Re-enact the story outdoors. Pretend as a group to be in the jungle. Do all the actions, and pretend to see/hear animals, rather like *We're going on a bear hunt*.
Physical play Physical Development – Movement and Space	Make a climbing frame into monkey bars (or a 'jungle'), by decorating and covering it with leaves and branches, either using paper or real materials. As children climb, crawl and swing, give lots of commentary on what they are doing, using these action words.
Listening Communication, Language and Literacy – Language for Communication Communication, Language and Literacy – Linking Sounds and Letters	Play listening lottos of jungle animals. Listen for noises around nursery and discuss whether they are 'noisy' or 'quiet'. Talk to the children about being 'noisy' or 'quiet' at group times. At singing time, sing and play musical instruments in a 'noisy' or 'quiet' way. Sing the song 'Walking through the jungle'.
Interactive display Creative Development – Developing Imagination and Imaginative Play	Photocopy and enlarge the jungle scene (page 184) and animals (page 185). Colour, cut, laminate and add Blu-Tac for the children to put in the jungle.

Photocopiable Resources
for
Walking in the Jungle

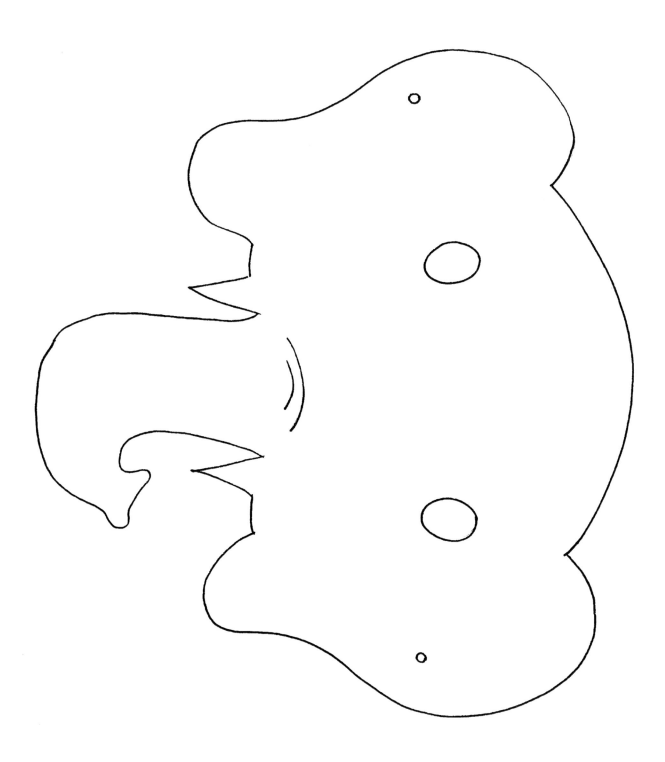

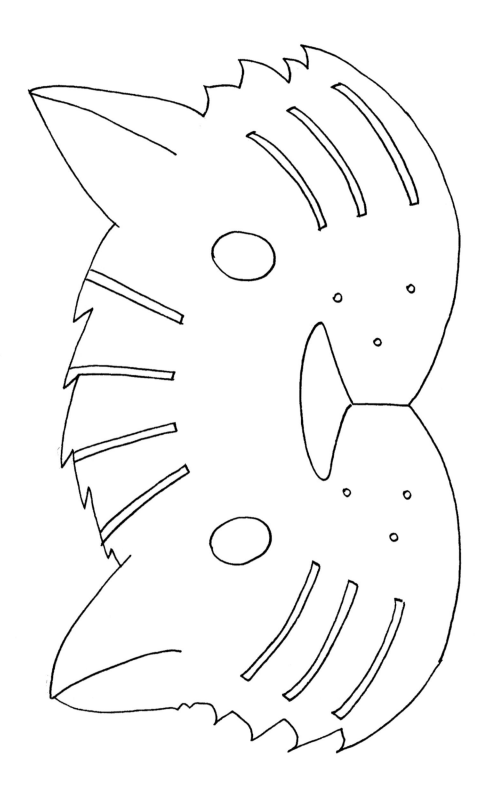

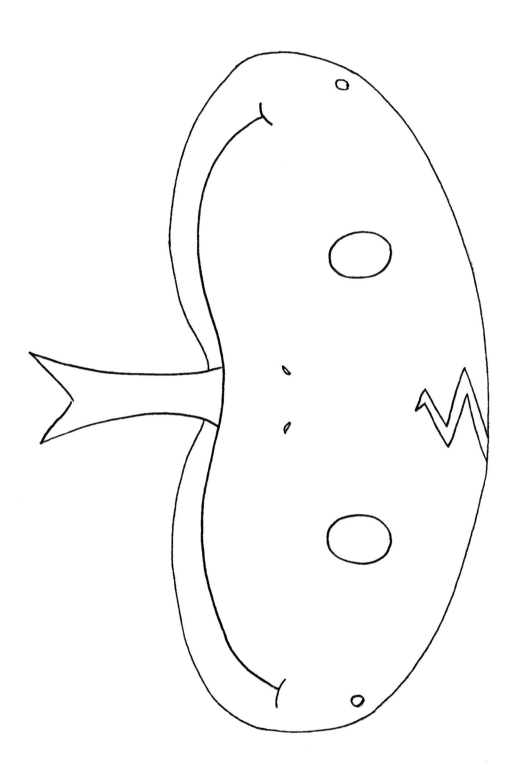

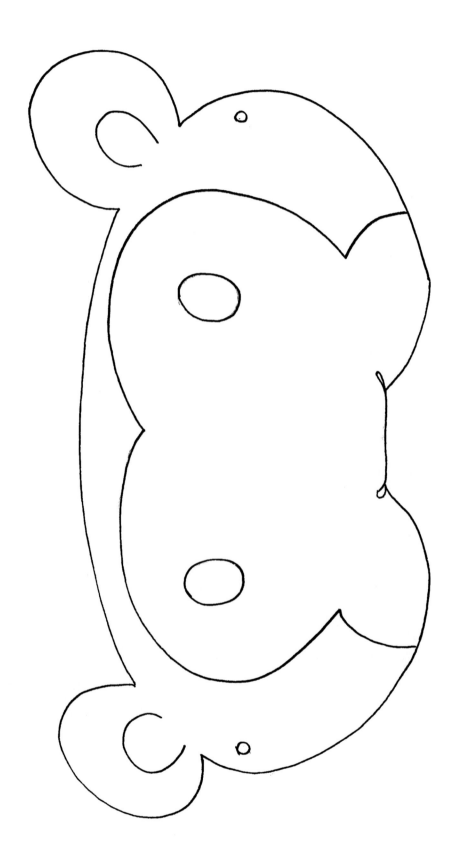

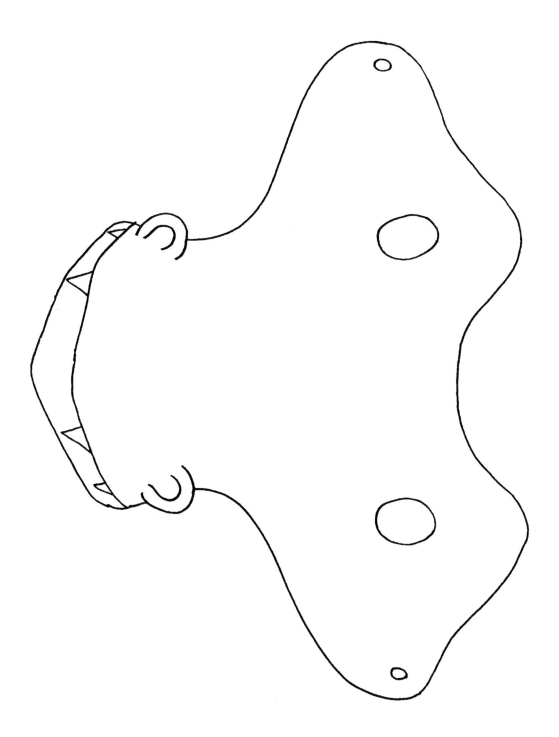

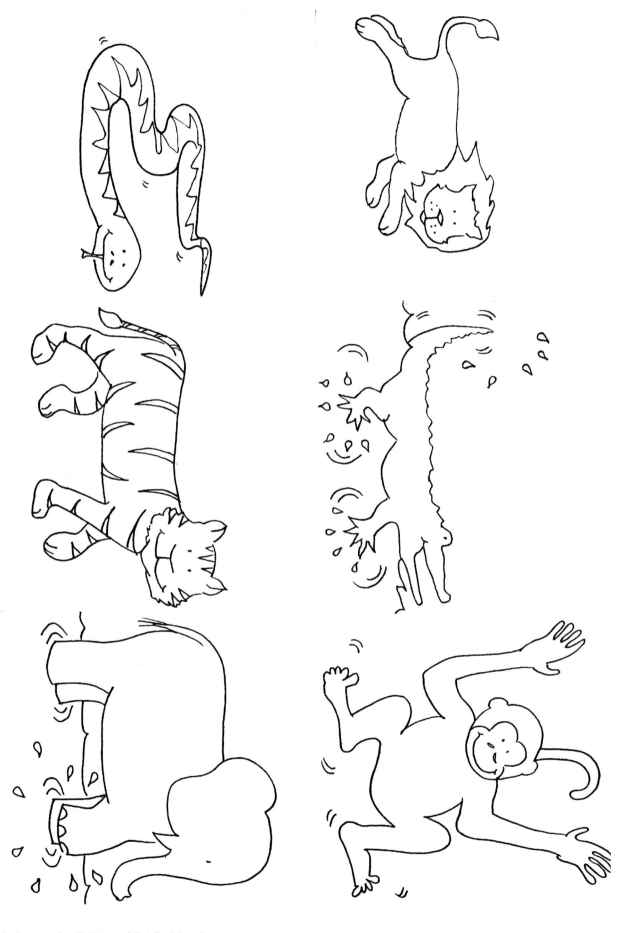

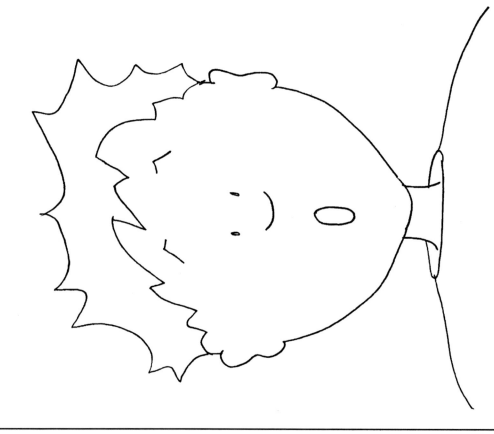

References

Alborough, J. (2007) *Washing Line*. London: Walker Books.

Bashir, A. and Scavuzzo, A. (1992) 'Children with language disorders: Natural history and academic success'. *Journal of Learning Difficulties*, 25 (1), 53-65.

Beitchman, J. H., Wilson, B., Johnson, C. J., Atkinson, L., Young, A., Adlaf, E., et al. (2001) 'Fourteen year follow-up of speech/language impaired children and control children: psychiatric outcome'. *Journal of the American Academy of Child and Adolescent Psychiatry*, 40 (1), 75-82.

Bercow Report (2008) *A Review of Services for Children and Young People (0-19) with Speech, Language and Communication Needs*. Nottingham: DCSF Publications.

Botting, N. (2007) Nuffield Education Seminar: 'Emotional and social health of young people with language impairments: What are the clinical and educational implications?' February 21st, The Nuffield Foundation.

Bryan, K. (2004) 'Preliminary study of the prevalence of speech and language difficulties in young offenders'. *International Journal of Language and Communication Disorders*, 39:3, 391-400.

Clegg, J., Hollis, C., Mawhood, L., Rutter, M., (2005) 'Developmental language disorders - a follow-up in later adult life. Cognitive, language and psychosocial outcomes'. *Journal of Child Psychology and Psychiatry* 46, 2, 128-149.

DCSF (2008) *The Early Years Foundation Stage*. Nottingham: DCSF Publications.

Hooper, S.J., Roberts J.E., Zeisel, S.A., and Poe, M. (2003) 'Core language predictors of behavioural functioning in early elementary school children: Concurrent and longitudinal findings'. *Behavioral Disorders*, 29 (1), 10-21.

Jerome A.C., Fujiki M., Brinton B., James S.L., (2002) 'Self esteem in children with specific language impairment'. *Journal of Speech Language and Hearing Research* Aug: 45 (4): 700-14.

Lacome, J. (1998) *Walking Through the Jungle*. London: Walker Books

Lindsay, G., Dockrell, J. and Strand, S. (2007)' Longitudinal patterns of behaviour problems in children with specific speech and language difficulties'. *British Journal of Educational Psychology* 77: 811-28.

Locke, A., and Ginsborg, J., (2003) 'Spoken language in the early years: the cognitive and language development of three to five year old children from socio-economically deprived backgrounds'. *Educational and Child Psychology* 20 68-79.

Redmond, S. M. and Rice, M.L. (2002) 'Stability of behavioural ratings of children with specific language impairment'. *Journal of Speech, Language and Hearing Research* 45, 190-201.

Sykes, J. (2002) *Dora's Eggs*. London: Little Tiger Press.

Young, A.R., Beitchman, J.H., Johnson, C., Douglas, L., Atkinson, L., Escobar, M., et al (2002) 'Young adult academic outcomes in a longitudinal sample of early identified language impaired and control children'. *Journal of child Psychology and Psychiatry*, 43(5), 635-645.